2nd Workshop on Semantic Deep Learning 2017 (SemDeep-2)

Montpellier, France
19 September 2017

Editors:

Dagmar Gromann
Thierry Declerck
Georg Heigl

ISBN: 978-1-5108-5300-3

Printed from e-media with permission by:

Curran Associates, Inc.
57 Morehouse Lane
Red Hook, NY 12571

CURRAN ASSOCIATES INC.
proceedings
.com

Some format issues inherent in the e-media version may also appear in this print version.

Printed by Curran Associates, Inc. (2017)

Association for Computational Linguistics
209 N. Eighth Street
Stroudsburg, Pennsylvania 18360

Phone: 1-570-476-8006
Fax: 1-570-476-0860

acl@aclweb.org

Additional copies of this publication are available from:

Curran Associates, Inc.
57 Morehouse Lane
Red Hook, NY 12571 USA
Phone: 845-758-0400
Fax: 845-758-2633
Email: curran@proceedings.com
Web: www.proceedings.com

Proceedings of the 2nd Workshop on Semantic Deep Learning (SemDeep-2)

September 19, 2017

Montpellier, France

Editors:

Dagmar Gromann, Thierry Declerck, Georg Heigl

Table of Contents

Proceedings of the 2nd Workshop on Semantic Deep Learning (SemDeep-2)

Workshop at the 12th International Conference on Computational Semantics (IWCS 2017)
Montpellier, France, September 19, 2017

ACL Anthology Proceedings
WS17-73

Organizing Committee

Georg Heigl	DFKI, Saarbrücken
Dagmar Gromann	IIIA-CSIC, Bellaterra
Thierry Declerck	DFKI, Saarbrücken

Program Committee

Kemo Adria	IIIA-CSIC, Barcelona
Luis Espinosa Anke	Savana, Madrid
Leon Derczynski,	University of Sheffield
Maarten Grachten	OFAI, Vienna
Stratos Kontopoulos	MKLAB, Thessaloniki
Brigitte Krenn	OFAI, Vienna
Enrico Santus	The Hong Kong Polytechnic University
Felix Sasaki	W3C & DFKI, Berlin
Vered Schwartz	Bar-Ilan University, Ramat Gan
Michael Spranger	Sony Computer Science Lab Inc., Tokyo
Arkaitz Zubiaga	University of Warwick

The Effect of Negative Sampling Strategy on Capturing Semantic Similarity in Document Embeddings

Marzieh Saeidi
marzieh@gluru.co

Ritwik Kulkarni
ritwik@gluru.co

Theodosia Togia
sia@gluru.co

Michele Sama
michele@gluru.co

Abstract

In many machine learning tasks, a model needs to be presented with both correct and incorrect examples during the training. For instance, given a query, a search engine can be trained to predict the relevant (positive) documents from irrelevant (negative) ones. While each query is associated with a handful of relevant documents, the number of irrelevant documents can be vast. This imbalance can bias a document retrieval model while the mere volume of irrelevant documents can result in long training times. In this paper, we show the affect of a tailored negative sampling on the performance of the Deep Structure Semantic Model (DSSM). We show that a naive random sampling method outperforms more sophisticated ways of selecting negative data.

1 Introduction

In many machine learning tasks, it is often the case that negative examples vastly outnumber positive ones. For instance, in a recommendation system, the number of items that a user has rated or purchased are far less than the total number of items available in the system. Similarly, in an answer retrieval task for the community question answering platforms, the number of relevant answers to a question is very low compared to the total number of available answers. To address this imbalance, negative examples are typically down-sampled in accordance with some criteria. The effect of negative sampling strategy has been studied across a range of machine learning and NLP tasks, with varying results (Wunsch et al., 2009; Ustalov et al., 2017; Bordes et al., 2014).

Sampling from the space of negative examples can be performed on the basis of three alternative intuitions, namely that negative examples should be: **i)** as similar as possible to positive examples to increase a model's discriminative power within small neighbourhoods **ii)** as different as possible to positive examples to avoid providing a model with conflicting information **iii)** representative of the entire space of negative examples, without preference for those similar or dissimilar to positive ones

The first intuition has led to *local sampling* methods (e.g. Wunsch et al. 2009), that is sampling from negative cases that are close to positive ones by some specified proximity measure, which can be either linguistically justified or based on vector space distances. The reason is to select or generate data that challenges a model's capacity to distinguish between seemingly similar items. The second intuition is associated with *distance sampling* (Wunsch et al., 2009), namely selecting negative cases that are as distinct as possible from positive ones in order to ensure the data are properly clustered in the vector space. The final intuition has led to *uniform sampling* methods, that is randomly sampling from the space of negative examples.

Adopting the correct negative sampling approach is largely task-dependent (see Section 5). Our research sought to determine the most suitable strategy for learning semantic similarity. In these particular experiments we focused on the widely adopted DSSM model (Huang et al., 2013) trained on the task of answer selection in the community question answering platform Yahoo! Answers.

Q1: *Help im scared! Dental problems?* two of my top adult teeth are a little bit loose, will i lose them? **A1:** If they are adult teeth, you dentist may be able to "tighten" them ...
Q2: *Do I need 2 dental bridges or just one huge one on my teeth?* I have 2 maryland bridges on my top teeth (the teeth on either side of my two top ... **A2:** I would suggest cantilever bridges will be more than enough ...
Q3: *Can Someone Give Me Links Proving Global Warming Real Or Not?* I believe global warming is real, but lately I realized I don't actually know that global warming is real ... **A3:** There are many reason why global warming can occur. From increased solar input to changes in atmospheric aerosol concentration to albedo and land use changes

Table 1: The first two QA pairs are under the category and subcategory *Health-Dental* category. The last QA is under *Environment-Global Warming*.

2 Model

We perform answer selection using the DSSM model Huang et al. (2013). The DSSM is a popular feedforward neural network for document retrieval.[1] It can be seen as a supervised version of latent semantic models (e.g. Latent Semantic Indexing Deerwester et al. (1990)), leveraging implicit document-query relevance judgments, originally from clickthrough data. The model non-linearly projects queries and documents to a reduced dimensionality semantic space which better captures dependencies between the dimensions of the original vector space. It does so by using an objective function which maximises the log probability of the relevant document (i.e. correct answer in the case of question answering) being the most similar. The input of DSSM is one query, one relevant document (positive example) and a number of irrelevant documents (negative examples), each one encoded as a bag of a character trigrams feature vector, as in the original paper.

2.1 Negative Sampling

In the dataset we used for these experiments, Yahoo! Answers, each question and answer group (QA) contains a question, a list of answers with one often flagged as the best answer. Additionally, each QA typically has a specified category and subcategory. In the experiments, given a question, we train the DSSM to maximise its ability to rank a relevant answer higher than any non-relevant one. This leads to a model whose representations of questions and answers belonging to the same topic are in the same neighbourhood. Ideally, a trained model should be not only capable of distinguishing *between* documents in different topics (i.e. to cluster question or answer vectors by their subject matter) but also *within* topics (i.e. to arrange vectors inside each topic in a way that reflects similarity of information need) , with similar questions and their relevant answers forming a sub-cluster within a topic cluster).

A straightforward way to improve the model's ability to discriminate across topics is to explicitly provide this information as input to the model during the training. However, increasing the model's discriminative power inside same-topic (i.e. category) neighbourhoods without compromising per subject clustering is more challenging. Table 1 shows examples of question from two different categories: Health-Dental and Environment- Global Warming. As we can see, QAs within the same category are more likely to have common and similar terms.

As one can assume, it may be easier for a model to distinguish among documents from different categories than those within the same category. Addressing this challenge might require a principled approach to negative sampling, that is deciding which positive and negative examples to provide the model with. For instance, if the model is fed with a politics-related question, what will be the most informative negative answers?

[1] We refer readers to this paper for more modelling details.

We can choose between random sampling, local sampling (e.g. providing negative examples from the same topic), distance sampling (e.g. providing negative answers outside the same topic, which have more pronounced differences with the correct response), or a combination of both.

In the experiments that follow, we compare the effect of two types of negative sampling on the performance of DSSM when topic information is provided to the model:

- Random sampling whereby negative examples are sampled uniformly from the space of all answers
- Refined sampling which is explained in details in Section 2.1.

In refined negative sampling, the model is presented with questions within the same category and subcategory (local sampling) as well as other categories (distance sampling) with a view to training a model capable of generating embeddings that are appropriately clustered not only across different categories, but also within each category. We use category and subcategory information available for each question in order to sample negative examples during the training. We sample from answers that belong to the same category, from answers that belong to the same subcategory and from answers that do not belong to the category of the question. We choose these proportions heuristically with 50% from inside the category (in particular, 20% from the subcategory and 30% from the entire category) and the remaining 50% from outside the category.

Figure 1 shows the number of QAs in each of the 26 categories in our dataset of 3 million QAs. As we can see, the number of QAs across different categories is not balanced. Using random sampling, we may never come across questions from the same category or subcategory for a given QA. This issue can be alleviated using refined sampling.

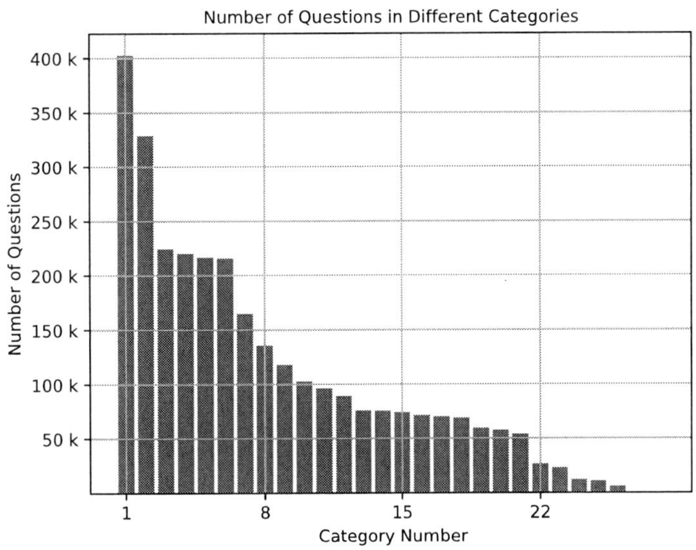

Figure 1: Number of QAs belonging to different 26 categories. Total number of QAs in our dataset is 3 million.

3 Experiments

We run our experiments on a corpus of Yahoo! Answers questions and answers, which contains over three million questions and answers.[2] Topic information is available by means of categories and subcategories logged by users when submitting a question. In our experiments, we use questions for which the

[2]`https://webscope.sandbox.yahoo.com`

following information is available: **i)** the 'best answer' chosen by the user (used as the positive example), **ii)** the category and subcategory label. Negative examples are chosen among other answers according to the preferred negative sampling strategy.

The authors of the DSSM paper (Huang et al., 2013) mention that they do not observe any significant difference by using different sampling strategies for the unclicked (irrelevant) documents. However, they do not discuss the negative sampling strategies. In this paper, we study the effect of a refined negative sampling strategy using the category information for the task of answer retrieval in the community question answering platforms. Intuitively, *random* sampling has limitations because random examples might not represent all the nuances of semantic dissimilarities.

We hypothesize that providing informative negative examples can help the model to learn more separable embeddings across different topics and within the same topic. Moreover, refined negative sampling may help the model to converge faster (since we provide it with information we believe is more vital from early on). We examine this hypothesis using the three experiments described below.

No Category In this experiment, even though we have access to the category information, in order to provide a baseline, no category information is provided during the training.[3] Since our refined negative sampling strategy uses category information, we only employ random negative sampling.

Category - Random Negative Sampling In this experiment, category and subcategory information is included in the representation of each document as one-hot vectors. Negative answers for each question are sampled randomly from the pool of all answers across all categories and subcategories.

Category - Refined Negative Sampling Similarly to the above experiment, here the category and subcategory information is included. However, instead of random negative sampling, we use the refined negative sampling method described in Section 2.1.

At test time, when searching for the correct answer, we search through two spaces. First, since the user has specified the category of the question, we use this category information to limit the search space by filtering for answers within the same category. This experiment tests the extent to which embeddings are separable within the same category. Second, we search through all the answers across all the categories. This is because we want to test whether the learned embeddings of questions are separable from the answers both globally and in the neighbourhood of the same category.

Evaluation We divide our dataset into train, dev and test sets. We use the dev set to decide when to stop the training and test set to report the evaluation results. While we run the experiments with a varying number of QAs in the training set, the dev and the test set each contain 20k QAs. We report results using Mean Recall@1, Mean Recall@5 and MRR (mean reciprocal rank) (Voorhees et al., 1999).

4 Results

In this section, we look at the performance of the model when trained **i)** with random negative sampling without the category information, tested on the two search spaces described above (*no_ctg* search within category and *no_ctg_all* for global search), **ii)** with random negative sampling and category information, tested on the same two search spaces (*ctg_rnd* and *ctg_rnd_all*) and using refined negative sampling with category information (*ctg_rfn* and *ctg_rfn_all*).

Figure 2 shows the performance of the models, in terms of Mean Recall@1. On the left hand side, the performance is illustrated as the number of negative samples during the training increases. This is done for the case when we search through the entire space (dashed line) and when we search through the category only (solid line). As expected, providing the model with category information increases retrieval performance. Among the models that use categories, the model trained with random negative sampling (blue line) outperforms the one trained with the refined negative sampling (green line). When searching only within the same category, the model with the random negative sampling performs considerably higher than the model trained using refined negative sampling. Moreover, unlike the model with refined

[3]It has been shown that adding category information improves the accuracy of finding the relevant answer in community question answering (Zhang et al., 2016). We also expect that including category information, will result in a better accuracy.

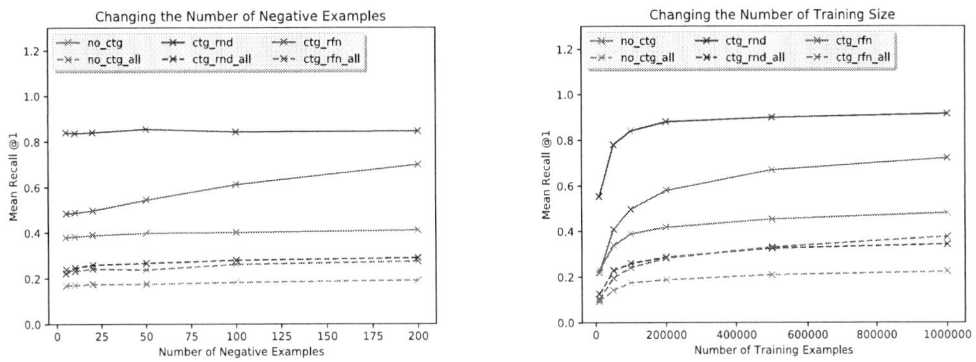

Figure 2: Performances of the models (in terms of *Mean Recall@1*) over the test set as the size of negative examples increases, with training size = 100k (top) and as the size of training examples increases, with negative size = 100 (bottom).

negative sampling, that does not reach a plateau, the model with the random negative sampling converges to the optimum performance without requiring a large number of negative examples during training.On the other hand, the performance of the model with the refined negative sampling does not reach a plateau even with 200 negative examples. On the right hand side of the figure, we see the performance of the models in terms of Mean Recall@1, as the size of training data increases. Similar to the previous figure, we can see that by adding category information (blue and green lines), search performance increases considerably. We see that the refined negative sampling has a negative effect on the performance of the DSSM. Further, the model with the random negative sampling reaches optimum performance using only 200k samples whereas the model that uses refined negative sampling does not reach a plateau even with 1m samples. Performance of the models in terms of Mean Recall@5 and MRR are illustrated in Figures 3 and 4. Similar patterns can be seen on these figures as well.

Further, by observing the dev loss during the training (Figure 5 in the Appendix), we can see that learning is stable across the epochs in the case of random sampling given the category information. However, when sampling is refined, there is a considerable amount of oscillation, which can reflect the model's effort to resolve the conflict between items in the same category being similar in some ways and different in others.

Overall, we observe that the refined negative sampling has a negative effect on the performance of the model, which is in line with the observation in Huang et al. (2013) for the document retrieval task.

The reason why refined sampling underperforms random sampling might be that DSSM mainly relies on text similarity in order to find relevant documents or answers. This is especially the case when working with longer documents such as QAs (as opposed to the experiments the authors of DSSm Huang et al. (2013) carried on document titles only) By providing negative examples from the same category, the model will see similar text patterns as negative examples (in the example in Table 1 the word "dental" has appeared in two questions within same category). This can possibly also explain why the loss fluctuates during training epochs when refined sampling is applied: the model is given conflicting information as to whether similar character trigrams are relevant to each other. However, as the number of negative examples or training examples increases, the model adjusts its weights so that similar terms in two documents make the documents relevant to each other.

4.1 Analysis

Figure 2 empirically demonstrates that the refined negative sampling results in performance loss compared to random sampling, when category information is provided. To analyse this behaviour more, we examine how the choice of negative sampling strategy (i.e. random or refined) affects the formation of vector space neighbourhoods whose vectors must share the same subject (e.g. 'Entertainment'). In par-

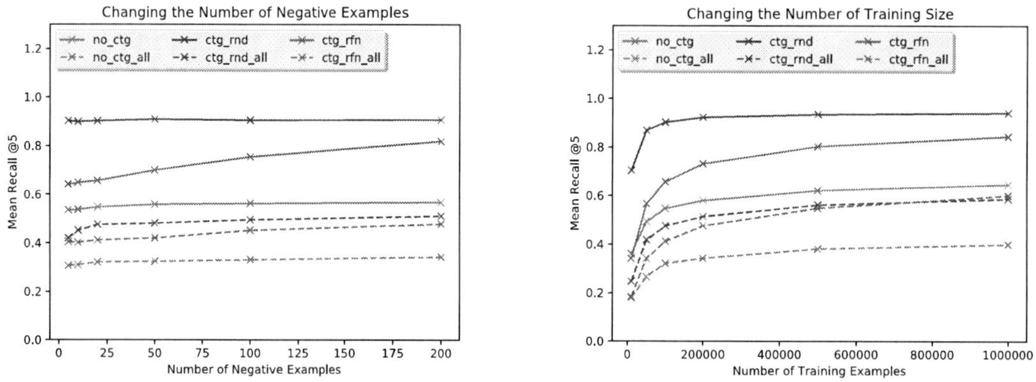

Figure 3: Performances of the models (*Mean Recall@5*) over the test set as the size of negative examples increases, training size = 100k (left) and as the size of training examples increases, negative size = 100 (right).

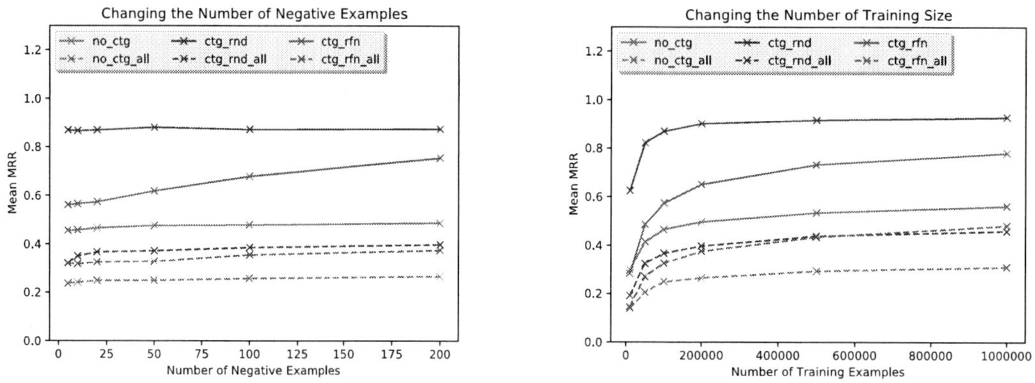

Figure 4: Performances of the models (*MRR*) over the test set as the size of negative examples increases, training size = 100k (left) and as the size of training examples increases, negative size = 100 (right).

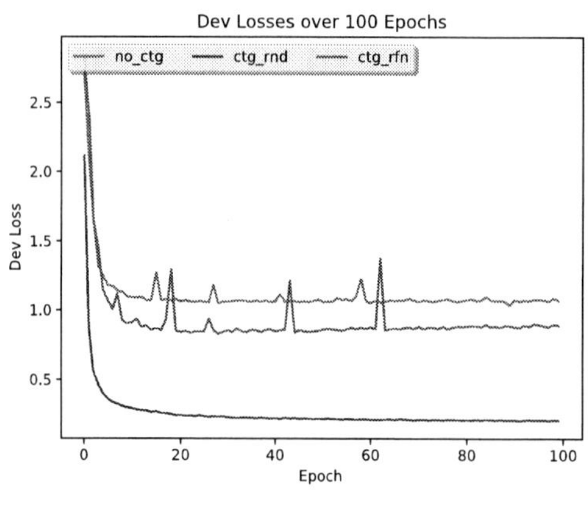

Figure 5: Dev loss during the training epochs.

ticular, we compare the two sampling approaches as to how similar their formed neighbourhoods are to the ideal clusters, which result from grouping vectors by their original Yahoo! Answers categories.

We start by generating embeddings using the DSSM for the two negative sampling strategies that include category information during training, namely, "Category with random negative sampling" ((*ctg_rnd* and *ctg_rnd_all* and "Category with refined negative sampling" (*ctg_rfn* and *ctg_rfn_all*). To explore the extent to which category information is encoded in the embeddings, we cluster the embeddings for each of the two cases independently and compare them with the ideal clusters, that are obtained by collecting together embeddings that have the same category. We perform k-means clustering with k set to the number of unique categories in the Yahoo! Answers dataset.

The two sets of clusters (one for each negative sampling strategy) are compared with the ideal Yahoo! Answers clusters using Mutual Information. If the clustering of embeddings agrees to a high degree with the Yahoo! Answers clusters then we can conclude that the category labels find a direct representation in the 128 dimensional embedding space, where the category information is among the principal components along which the questions are arranged. Mutual information, which here is used to quantify the dependence between each of the two sets of clusters with the ideal set (i.e. Yahoo! Answers clusters), can be calculated as follows:

$$I(X,Y) = H(X) + H(Y) - H(X;Y)$$

where $I(X,Y)$ is the mutual information between sets X and Y, $H(X)$ is the entropy of the set X, while $H(X;Y)$ is the joint entropy of the sets X and Y.

	YC-Emb_R	YC-Emb_N
I	0.492	0.365
I/H(YC)	0.118	0.087

Table 2: Mutual information between Yahoo! Answers clusters and embedding clusters with refined negative sampling ($YC - Emb\_N$) or embedding clusters with random negative sampling ($YC - Emb\_R$)

The very low mutual information between the embeddings and Yahoo clusters for both with and without refined negative sampling (Table 2) indicates that the category labels do not have a significant influence on how the embeddings are arranged in the vector space. We can observe that the clusters formed when DSSM is trained with random negative sampling (Emb_R) have higher mutual information with the ideal Yahoo! Answers clusters compared to that of refined negative sampling clusters (Emb_N) and Yahoo.This adds to the notion developed from figures 2, 3 and 4 that refined negative sampling disrupts the learning across and within category examples.

5 Related work

Mikolov et al. Mikolov et al. (2013) introduce "negative sampling" as a way of approximating the calculation of softmax over the entire vocabulary for each forward step. The effect of negative sampling strategy has been studied across a range of NLP tasks, with varying results. Wunsch et al. (2009) perform local sampling for anaphora resolution by selecting non-anaphoric pairs from sentences surrounding anaphoric pairs (i.e. positive data). In another experiment, they use as negative examples the ones misclassified by a classifier trained on positive data only. However, they obtain their best results using random sampling. Similarly, for the task of hypernymy extraction, Ustalov et al. (2017) boost the performance of their system by selecting a false hypernym for a word from the neighbourhood of the correct hypernym. They report a drop in performance when random sampling is applied. Bordes et al. (2014) obtain negative entity-relation-entity triples for open question answering by partially corrupting positive ones, creating negative examples that are more challenging for a model to discriminate. Logacheva et al. (2015) improve their machine translation system by generating negative examples from variations of the positive ones. For the task of co-reference resolution, Zhekova (2011) achieves improvements by adjusting the ratio of positive to negative examples. Negative sampling has also been investigated in the context of discourse relation extraction (Li and Nenkova, 2014) and classification of caused motion constructions (Hwang and Palmer, 2015).

6 Conclusions

In this paper, we examine the impact of a refined negative sampling on the performance of the Deep Structured Semantic Model (Huang et al., 2013) when applied to an answer retrieval task in community question answering. We found that random sampling, albeit less sophisticated, is a more reliable method for providing negative examples to DSSM, as had originally been observed for the task of web search. As a future experiment, the same negative sampling techniques can be used with a model other than DSSM. This can shed light on whether this effect is due to the model's inherent limitations in learning semantic information, which restrict its ability to handle more subtle negative examples or whether it is a more general trend in the task of answer retrieval for community question answering.

References

Bordes, A., J. Weston, and N. Usunier (2014). Open Question Answering with Weakly Supervised Embedding Models. *Ecml*, 165–180.

Deerwester, S., S. T. Dumais, G. W. Furnas, T. K. Landauer, and R. Harshman (1990). Indexing by latent semantic analysis. *Journal of the American society for information science 41*(6), 391.

Huang, P.-s., N. M. A. Urbana, X. He, J. Gao, L. Deng, A. Acero, and L. Heck (2013). Learning Deep Structured Semantic Models for Web Search using Clickthrough Data. *the 22nd ACM international conference on Conference on information & knowledge management*, 2333–2338.

Hwang, D. J. and M. Palmer (2015). Identification of Caused Motion Construction. *Proceedings of the Fourth Joint Conference on Lexical and Computational Semantics*, 51–60.

Li, J. J. and A. Nenkova (2014). Addressing Class Imbalance for Improved Recognition of Implicit Discourse Relations. *Proceedings of the 15th Annual Meeting of the Special Interest Group on Discourse and Dialogue (SIGDIAL)* (June), 142–150.

Logacheva, V. and L. Specia (2015). The role of artificially generated negative data for quality estimation of machine translation. *18th Annual Conference of the European Association for Machine Translation*, 51 - 58.

Mikolov, T., K. Chen, G. Corrado, and J. Dean (2013). Distributed Representations of Words and Phrases and their Compositionality. *Nips*, 1–9.

Ustalov, D., N. Arefyev, C. Biemann, and A. Panchenko (2017). Negative Sampling Improves Hypernymy Extraction Based on Projection Learning. *2*, 543–550.

Voorhees, E. M. et al. (1999). The trec-8 question answering track report. In *Trec*, Volume 99, pp. 77–82.

Wunsch, H., S. Kübler, and R. Cantrell (2009). Instance Sampling Methods for Pronoun Resolution. *Proceedings of the International Conference on Recent Advances in Natural Language Processing*, 478–483.

Zhang, K., W. Wu, F. Wang, M. Zhou, and Z. Li (2016). Learning distributed representations of data in community question answering for question retrieval. In *Proceedings of the Ninth ACM International Conference on Web Search and Data Mining*, pp. 533–542. ACM.

Zhekova, D. (2011). Zhekova - Instance Sampling for Multilingual Coreference Resolution. 7(September), 150–155.

Building Graph Representations of Deep Vector Embeddings

Dario Garcia-Gasulla
Barcelona Supercomputing Center (BSC)
dario.garcia@bsc.es

Armand Vilalta
Barcelona Supercomputing Center (BSC)
armand.vilalta@bsc.es

Ferran Parés
Barcelona Supercomputing Center (BSC)
ferran.pares@bsc.es

Jonatan Moreno
Barcelona Supercomputing Center (BSC)
jonatan.moreno@bsc.es

Eduard Ayguadé
Barcelona Supercomputing Center (BSC)
Universitat Politècnica de Catalunya
eduard.ayguade@bsc.es

Jesús Labarta
Barcelona Supercomputing Center (BSC)
Universitat Politècnica de Catalunya
jesus.labarta@bsc.es

Ulises Cortés
Barcelona Supercomputing Center (BSC)
Universitat Politècnica de Catalunya
ia@cs.upc.edu

Toyotaro Suzumura
Barcelona Supercomputing Center (BSC)
IBM T.J. Watson
tsuzumura@us.ibm.com

Abstract

Patterns stored within pre-trained deep neural networks compose large and powerful descriptive languages that can be used for many different purposes. Typically, deep network representations are implemented within vector embedding spaces, which enables the use of traditional machine learning algorithms on top of them. In this short paper we propose the construction of a graph embedding space instead, introducing a methodology to transform the knowledge coded within a deep convolutional network into a topological space (*i.e.*, a network). We outline how such graph can hold data instances, data features, relations between instances and features, and relations among features. Finally, we introduce some preliminary experiments to illustrate how the resultant graph embedding space can be exploited through graph analytics algorithms.

1 Introduction

Deep learning models build large and rich data representations by finding complex patterns within large and high-dimensional datasets. At the end of a deep learning training procedure, the learnt model can be understood as a data representation language, where the pattern learnt by each neuron within the deep model represents a word of such language. Extracting and reusing the patterns learnt by a deep neural network (DNN) is a subfield of deep learning known as transfer learning. Transfer learning from a pre-trained DNN can be used to initialize the training of a second DNN from a non-random state, improving performance over randomly initialized networks [22, 2, 10], and also enabling the training of DNNs for domains with limited amount of data [8, 20]. These two settings, where the purpose of the transfer learning process is to train a second DNN, are cases of transfer learning for fine tuning. A different purpose of transfer learning is to extract deep representations so that alternative machine learning methods can be run on top of those. This is commonly known as *transfer learning for feature extraction*, and is the main topic of this paper.

Extracted DNN representations are typically implemented through vectors, where the length of the vector equals to the number of neural features being used. These vector embedding spaces have been used to feed classifiers based on the instance-attribute paradigm (*e.g.*, Support Vector Machines) [1, 7]. Instead, in this paper we propose a *graph* based representation of those same embeddings spaces, with the goal of running a different family of algorithms; those based on the instance-instance paradigm, such as community detection algorithms. Graph or network based algorithms focus on the associations among instances to find topologically coherent patterns. These are significantly different from the patterns that can be found using algorithms focused on the associations among instances and attributes. This paper describes a methodology for building a graph representation of neural network embeddings (in §2), and reports the performance of a community detection algorithm processing the resultant graph (in §3).

2 Graph Representation of Vector Embeddings

Vector embeddings are often built by capturing the output of a single layer close to the output of a deep convolutional neural network (CNN), typically a fully-connected layer [18, 9, 5, 11, 16]. However, earlier layers can also be useful for characterizing data, particularly when this data is not strongly related with the data that was used for pre-training the model [1]. Another difference between later layers and the rest in a typical CNN trained for classification is that layers close to the output exhibit a strongly discriminative behavior, activating sporadically and in a crisp manner (either strongly activating or not at all). In contrast, neurons of layers further from the output show a more descriptive behavior, activating frequently and in a fuzzy way [6].

In this paper we generate a graph representation which captures data properties in a topological space (*i.e.*, through vertices and their associations). Using a single layer embedding for that purpose would result in a rather poor topology, as fully-connected layers represent but a portion of all patterns learnt by the DNN, and only a small subset of neurons activate for each data instance. To guarantee that the graph representation contains a topology rich enough as to empower network analysis algorithms we use the full-network embedding [7], which produces a vector embedding including all convolutional and fully-connected layers of a CNN. This results in a much larger embedding space (composed by tens of thousands of dimensions), allowing us to generate larger and richer graphs.

Next we briefly introduce the full-network embedding, and at the end of this section we describe how we generate a graph to capture the embedding space within its topology.

2.1 Full-network Embedding

The full-network embedding (FNE) generates a representation of an input data instance by capturing the activations it produces at every convolutional and fully-connected layer within a CNN. In order to integrate the features found at layers of different depth, size and nature, the FNE includes a set of processing steps. An overview of these can be seen in Figure 1.

After the extraction of activations, the FNE applies a spatial average pooling on the activations coming from convolutional layers. As a result, neurons of convolutional layers will generate a single value in the embedding (as neurons from fully-connected layers do). After the spatial pooling, the FNE includes a feature standardization step. The goal of this transformation is to normalize the values of the different neurons, so that each neuron has a coherent range of activations regardless of its type or location within the CNN. Otherwise, the activations from the layers close to the output would dominate the representation, as neurons from these layers typically activate with much more strength.

Finally, the FNE discretizes features, mapping all values to either -1, 0 or 1. This process reduces noise and regularizes the embedding space. In the FNE, this discretization is done with a pair of constant thresholds $(-0.25, 0.15)$ which determine if a feature is relevant by presence (1 implies an abnormally high activation) or is relevant by absence (-1 implies an abnormally low activation) for a given input data instance [7]. In our experiments we set more demanding thresholds $(-2.0, 2.0)$, to make sure that the degree of sparsity of the graph is appropriate for network analysis methods.

2.2 Graph Representation

The FNE generates a vector representation of each data input, where feature values are either -1, 0 or 1. Those values represent the relevance of a specific neural filter for a given data input, indicating feature

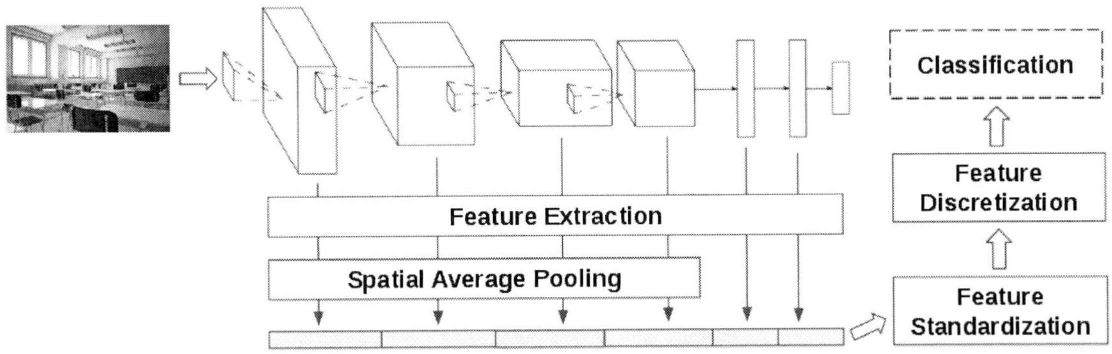

Figure 1: Overview of the Full-network embedding generation workflow.

relevance by absence, feature irrelevance, and feature relevance by presence, respectively. In this paper we consider building a topology based representation (*i.e.*, a graph) of such embedding, and processing it through algorithms exploiting instance-instance relations (*e.g.*, community detection) to exploit the information encoded topologically.

2.2.1 Vertices

Let us start defining what composes the vertices (V) of our graph representation G. From the discrete three-valued full-network embedding we extract both data instances (*e.g.*, images of a dataset) and model features (*i.e.*, neural filters of the CNN). Each data instance is represented in the graph G as a unique vertex (of type image vertex or V_i). Features however, may be relevant by presence or by absence. We choose to capture this dichotomy by creating two vertices in the graph for each feature; one of those vertices will represent the relevant activation of the feature (positive feature vertex or V_f^+), while the other will represent the relevant lack of activation of the feature (negative feature vertex or V_f^-). As a result, the number of image vertices in the graph ($|V_i|$) will be equal to the number of input data images, while the number of positive and negative feature vertices ($|V_f^+|$ and $|V_f^-|$ separately) will be equal to the number of features in the original vector embedding.

2.2.2 Image-Feature Edges

Let us now define the edges (E) of our graph representation G. The implementation of edges between image vertices and feature vertices (E_{if}) is straight-forward. We add an edge between a vertex image v_i and a positive feature vertex v_f^+ when the corresponding value in the full-network embedding is 1. Analogously, we add an edge between a vertex image v_i and a negative feature vertex v_f^- when the corresponding value in the full-network embedding is -1. Edges between image vertices and positive feature vertices indicate that the occurrence of the feature is relevant for describing the image, while edges between image vertices and negative feature vertices indicate that the no occurrence of the feature is relevant for describing the image. Feature values of 0 identify irrelevancy, which is why these are not coded into the graph.

2.2.3 Feature-Feature Edges

One of the benefits of using a graph-based representation for the embedding is that, unlike vector representations, it allows us to extend the embedding space to include feature-feature relations. In the graph this corresponds to the creation of edges between feature vertices (E_{ff}). To identify relations between features we consider the weights ($\mathcal{W}$) of the pre-trained CNN. If the weight associating a neuron f_{l+1} with a neuron from the previous layer f_l ($\mathcal{W}(f_{l+1}, f_l)$) is abnormally high in the context of all weights of f_{l+1} with the previous layer ($\mathcal{W}(f_{l+1}, F_l)$), there exists a positive correlation between both neurons.

Similarly, if $\mathcal{W}(f_{l+1}, f_l)$ is abnormally low in the context of $\mathcal{W}(f_{l+1}, F_l)$, there exists a negative correlation between neurons f_{l+1} and f_l. To identify what counts as abnormally high or abnormally low, we compute the mean (μ) and the standard deviation (σ) of the weights that associate a feature f_{l+1} from a given layer with every feature from the previous layer $f_i \in F_l$ (in the case of convolutional filters we previously sum all the weights of the receptive field). If the weight associating f_{l+1} with one of the features of the previous layer is above that mean a given number of standard deviations, then such relation is abnormally high (see Equation 1). An abnormally low relation is defined analogously.

We implement positive correlations in the graph by adding an edge between the positive feature vertex of f_l and the positive feature vertex of f_{l+1} ($e_{ff}(v^+_{f_l}, v^+_{f_{l+1}})$), and another edge between the negative feature vertex of f_l and the negative feature vertex of f_{l+1} ($e_{ff}(v^-_{f_l}, v^-_{f_{l+1}})$). Negative correlations are implemented by adding an edge between the positive feature vertex of f_l and the negative feature vertex of f_{l+1} ($e_{ff}(v^+_{f_l}, v^-_{f_{l+1}})$), and another edge between the negative feature vertex of f_l and the positive feature vertex of f_{l+1} ($e_{ff}(v^-_{f_l}, v^+_{f_{l+1}})$).

$$\begin{aligned}
\{e_{ff}(v^+_{f_l}, v^+_{f_{l+1}}), e_{ff}(v^-_{f_l}, v^-_{f_{l+1}})\} \in E_{ff} \quad \text{iff} \quad \mathcal{W}(f_{l+1}, f_l) > \mu(\mathcal{W}(f_{l+1}, F_l)) + \sigma(\mathcal{W}(f_{l+1}, F_l)) * k \\
\{e_{ff}(v^+_{f_l}, v^-_{f_{l+1}}), e_{ff}(v^-_{f_l}, v^+_{f_{l+1}})\} \in E_{ff} \quad \text{iff} \quad \mathcal{W}(f_{l+1}, f_l) < \mu(\mathcal{W}(f_{l+1}, F_l)) - \sigma(\mathcal{W}(f_{l+1}, F_l)) * k
\end{aligned} \tag{1}$$

The parameter k of Equation1 regulates the sparsity of feature-feature edges. A higher k value will only accept edges between very strongly connected pairs of neurons, as the associated weights must be a larger number of standard deviations above the mean. In all our experiments we set k to 1.5.

At this point we can finally define our graph representation as $G = (V, E)$ where $E = E_{if} \cup E_{ff}$ and $V = V_i \cup V^+_f \cup V^-_f$.

3 Experiments

To evaluate our graph representation of the deep embedding space we use the VGG16 CNN architecture [21], pre-trained on the ImageNet [17] dataset. We process four different datasets through this pre-trained model. Details on the datasets are shown in Table 1:

- The MIT Indoor Scene Recognition dataset [15] (*mit67*) consists of different indoor scenes to be classified in 67 categories.
- The Oxford Flower dataset [12] (*flowers102*) is a fine-grained dataset consisting of 102 flower categories.
- The Describable Textures Dataset [4] (*textures*) is a database of textures categorized according to a list of 47 terms inspired from human perception.
- The Oulu Knots dataset [19] (*wood*) contains knot images from spruce wood, classified according to Nordic Standards.

For each of the images of those datasets we obtain the full-network embedding. In the case of the VGG16 architecture, the embedding generates vectors of 12,416 features. Based on those, we build the graph representation, as previously described.

We explore the graph-representation by running a community detection algorithm on top of it. Particularly, we use the Fluid Communities (FluidC) algorithm [13]. We chose this algorithm because its based on the efficient label propagation methodology while outperforming the traditional LPA algorithm, because it allows us to specify the number of clusters we wish to find, and because it can be easily adapted to the specific needs of our experiments. These specific needs regard mostly cluster initialization and maintainance. Since the graph is composed by both images and features vertices, but only images have an associated label, clusters should be evaluated considering only the image vertices found in a final community. For this same reason, we must ensure that all communities found contain at least one image

Table 1: Properties of all datasets computed

Dataset	#Images	#Classes	#Images per class
mit67	6,700	67	100
flowers102	8,189	102	40 - 258
textures	5,640	47	120
wood	438	7	14 - 179

Table 2: Properties of the graphs built from the deep embedding spaces, and quality of the communities found by the FluidC algorithm measured in NMI and AMI.

Dataset	*mit67*	*flowers102*	*textures*	*wood*
$\|V\|$	30,186	33,010	30,459	25,259
$\|E\|$	8,396,939	9,654,464	8,561,314	5,610,832
NMI	0.44	0.54	0.42	0.26
AMI	0.36	0.46	0.37	0.20

vertex. This is done by modifying the FluidC algorithm, forcing it to initialize communities on image vertices, and by making sure that a community contains at least one image vertex at all times.

We measure the quality of the found clusters by measuring the similarity between the found communities and the original dataset labels. We use both the normalized mutual information measure (NMI) and the adjusted mutual information (AMI). The properties of the graph generated for each dataset and the performance results are shown in Table 2.

All experiments were done using the VGG16 model pre-trained on ImageNet2012, freely available online. The feature extraction process was done with Caffe. The execution of the graph algorithm was done using NetworkX v2.0, which includes FluidC.

4 Related Work

The relation between graphs and deep neural networks have been previously explored, but most contributions do so from a different perspective. While our proposal is to obtain a graph representation of the embedding produced by a CNN when processing an image, most related work focuses on training DNNs for processing graph data. For example, DeepWalk [14] uses random walks in a graph (*e.g.*, Flickr or YouTube networks) to feed a SkipGram model, and then evaluate community detection methods on those graphs. Similarly to DeepWalk, the work of Cao et al. [3] also processes graphs as input, but it uses a probabilistic approach on weighted graphs to feed an autoencoder. In contrast, we are performing community detection on a dataset of images, something that, to the best of our knowledge, had not been done before.

5 Conclusions

The presented methodology is a first step towards building graph-based representations of deep CNN embeddings. We detail how to include in such a graph both images and features, and how to topologically codify image-feature and feature-feature relations. By doing so we make deep knowledge available to a large set of learning algorithms (network analysis tools) which may exploit those representations in a completely different manner.

The results reported are encouraging, as a topology based algorithm such as FluidC is capable of identifying relevant communities of images using only topological information. The clusters that can be found through network analysis tools are significantly different than the clusters that can be found through more traditional algorithms (*e.g.*, Kmeans) running on a vector representation. Indeed, while algorithms like FluidC exploit the paths among vertices, algorithms like Kmeans are based on distance measures which can hardly integrate the information of all possible paths in a graph. The possibility of running a different type of algorithms makes this novel approach interesting, as it opens the door at exploiting and reusing the knowledge coded within deep pre-trained neural models in a completely new way. This is but a small step towards a better understanding of deep representations, and how to exploit all the knowledge these encode for a wider variety of purposes.

6 Future Work

The experiments shown in this paper are highly exploratory, with the purpose of validating the feasibility of the hypothesis (*i.e.*, that deep neural representations can be implemented as a graph coherently). Analytically, it would be desirable to compare the performance of the proposed approach with alternatives, such as applying a clustering algorithm on the original vector embeddings. However, clustering evaluation is a controversial topic, as there is not a single solution which may be considered to be the universal ground truth.

A more relevant evaluation of the approach should be based on an analysis of the semantics captured by the graph. For that purpose we are considering the extension of the model to include directed edges, weighted edges, and ontological relations. By doing so one could execute inference methods on top of the representation, and measure how rich and usable the semantics captured in the graph actually are.

Acknowledgements

This work is partially supported by the Joint Study Agreement no. W156463 under the IBM/BSC Deep Learning Center agreement, by the Spanish Government through Programa Severo Ochoa (SEV-2015-0493), by the Spanish Ministry of Science and Technology through TIN2015-65316-P project, by the Generalitat de Catalunya (contracts 2014-SGR-1051), and by the Core Research for Evolutional Science and Technology (CREST) program of Japan Science and Technology Agency (JST).

References

[1] Azizpour, H., A. S. Razavian, J. Sullivan, A. Maki, and S. Carlsson (2016). Factors of transferability for a generic convnet representation. *IEEE Transactions on Pattern Analysis and Machine Intelligence 38*(9), 1790–1802.

[2] Branson, S., G. Van Horn, S. Belongie, and P. Perona (2014). Bird species categorization using pose normalized deep convolutional nets. *arXiv preprint arXiv:1406.2952*.

[3] Cao, S., W. Lu, and Q. Xu (2016). Deep neural networks for learning graph representations. In *AAAI*, pp. 1145–1152.

[4] Cimpoi, M., S. Maji, I. Kokkinos, S. Mohamed, and A. Vedaldi (2014). Describing textures in the wild. In *Proceedings of the IEEE Conference on Computer Vision and Pattern Recognition*, pp. 3606–3613.

[5] Donahue, J., Y. Jia, O. Vinyals, J. Hoffman, N. Zhang, E. Tzeng, and T. Darrell (2014). Decaf: A deep convolutional activation feature for generic visual recognition. In *Icml*, Volume 32, pp. 647–655.

[6] Garcia-Gasulla, D., F. Parés, A. Vilalta, J. Moreno, E. Ayguadé, J. Labarta, U. Cortés, and T. Suzumura (2017). On the behavior of convolutional nets for feature extraction. *arXiv preprint arXiv:1703.01127*.

[7] Garcia-Gasulla, D., A. Vilalta, F. Parés, J. Moreno, E. Ayguadé, J. Labarta, U. Cortés, and T. Suzumura (2017). An out-of-the-box full-network embedding for convolutional neural networks. *arXiv preprint arXiv:1705.07706*.

[8] Ge, W. and Y. Yu (2017). Borrowing treasures from the wealthy: Deep transfer learning through selective joint fine-tuning. *arXiv preprint arXiv:1702.08690*.

[9] Gong, Y., L. Wang, R. Guo, and S. Lazebnik (2014). Multi-scale orderless pooling of deep convolutional activation features. In *European conference on computer vision*, pp. 392–407. Springer.

[10] Liu, C., Y. Cao, Y. Luo, G. Chen, V. Vokkarane, and Y. Ma (2016). Deepfood: Deep learning-based food image recognition for computer-aided dietary assessment. In *International Conference on Smart Homes and Health Telematics*, pp. 37–48. Springer.

[11] Mousavian, A. and J. Kosecka (2015). Deep convolutional features for image based retrieval and scene categorization. *arXiv preprint arXiv:1509.06033*.

[12] Nilsback, M.-E. and A. Zisserman (2008). Automated flower classification over a large number of classes. In *Computer Vision, Graphics & Image Processing, 2008. ICVGIP'08. Sixth Indian Conference on*, pp. 722–729. IEEE.

[13] Parés, F., D. Garcia-Gasulla, A. Vilalta, J. Moreno, E. Ayguadé, J. Labarta, U. Cortés, and T. Suzumura (2017). Fluid communities: A community detection algorithm. *arXiv preprint arXiv:1703.09307*.

[14] Perozzi, B., R. Al-Rfou, and S. Skiena (2014). Deepwalk: Online learning of social representations. In *Proceedings of the 20th ACM SIGKDD international conference on Knowledge discovery and data mining*, pp. 701–710. ACM.

[15] Quattoni, A. and A. Torralba (2009). Recognizing indoor scenes. In *Computer Vision and Pattern Recognition, 2009. CVPR 2009. IEEE Conference on*, pp. 413–420. IEEE.

[16] Ren, R., T. Hung, and K. C. Tan (2017). A generic deep-learning-based approach for automated surface inspection. *IEEE Transactions on Cybernetics*.

[17] Russakovsky, O., J. Deng, H. Su, J. Krause, S. Satheesh, S. Ma, Z. Huang, A. Karpathy, A. Khosla, M. Bernstein, et al. (2015). Imagenet large scale visual recognition challenge. *International Journal of Computer Vision 115*(3), 211–252.

[18] Sharif Razavian, A., H. Azizpour, J. Sullivan, and S. Carlsson (2014). Cnn features off-the-shelf: an astounding baseline for recognition. In *Proceedings of the IEEE Conference on Computer Vision and Pattern Recognition Workshops*, pp. 806–813.

[19] Silvén, O., M. Niskanen, and H. Kauppinen (2003). Wood inspection with non-supervised clustering. *Machine Vision and Applications 13*(5), 275–285.

[20] Simon, M. and E. Rodner (2015). Neural activation constellations: Unsupervised part model discovery with convolutional networks. In *Proceedings of the IEEE International Conference on Computer Vision*, pp. 1143–1151.

[21] Simonyan, K. and A. Zisserman (2014). Very deep convolutional networks for large-scale image recognition. *arXiv preprint arXiv:1409.1556*.

[22] Xu, Z., S. Huang, Y. Zhang, and D. Tao (2015). Augmenting strong supervision using web data for fine-grained categorization. In *Proceedings of the IEEE International Conference on Computer Vision*, pp. 2524–2532.

Class disjointness constraints as specific objective functions in neural network classifiers

François Scharffe
Axon Research
fscharffe@axon.com

Abstract

Increasing performance of deep learning techniques on computer vision tasks like object detection has led to systems able to detect a large number of classes of objects. Most deep learning models use simple unstructured labels and assume that any domain knowledge will be learned from the data. However when the domain is complex and the data limited, it may be useful to use domain knowledge encoded in an ontology to guide the learning process. In this paper, we conduct experiments to introduce constraints into the training process of a neural network. We show that explicitly modeling a disjointness axiom between a set of classes as a specific objective function leads to reducing violations for this constraint, while also reducing the overall classification error. This opens a way to import domain knowledge modeled in an ontology into a deep learning process.

1 Introduction

As deep learning research progresses, efforts are made to add structure to the set of labels used as annotation data. This seems a logical step as the number of labels in object classification tasks becomes larger. For example the ImageNet challenge (Russakovsky et al., 2015) in its 2017 edition invites system to localize objects in 1000 categories, detect 200 types of objects in images, and detect 20 types of objects in videos.[1] However little about the organization of these classes is provided. Models are expected to implicitly acquire the knowledge that, for example, a person has two legs and a car four wheels from the training examples provided as part of the dataset. What works on a controlled dataset in an academic challenge task might however be less practical in a real world example where annotated data can be scarce, and the modeled domain vast and complex.

The work presented in this paper is part of a larger project for automating the understanding of body worn camera footage in a law enforcement setting. The goal is to provide annotations that will facilitate the manual footage reviewing process that is mandatory across many agencies. We train deep learning models to categorize videos by their type, for example a Traffic Stop, or a Pedestrian Stop; and to give annotations indicating the type of event ongoing at a specific time segment, for example an Officer Driving, or a Handcuffing. The illustration below shows an example timeline our tool generates on an unseen video.

In parallel to developing models able to capture the specificities of this visual domain, we develop an ontology modeling this domain. Type of detections are represented as classes modeled in RDFS and OWL (Dean et al., 2004). There are three higher level classes for topics, segments, and objects that represent different levels of granularity: topics apply to a whole video, segments apply to a scene in a video that may vary from a few seconds to many minutes, and objects can be detected at any point in the video.

Because of legal and privacy concerns, and because of the cost of annotation, our training data set is limited to a few hundred videos. This results in the need for models able to learn from small training sets. In particular, we would like to be able to reflect the constraints modeled in the ontology into the neural network training process, so that this additional knowledge helps the neural network converge faster and compensates for the small training set. We indeed assume that if a much larger training set would be available, the constraints implicitly modeled in the annotations could be learned by the neural network.

[1] `http://image-net.org/challenges/LSVRC/2017/` retrieved on 07/05/2017

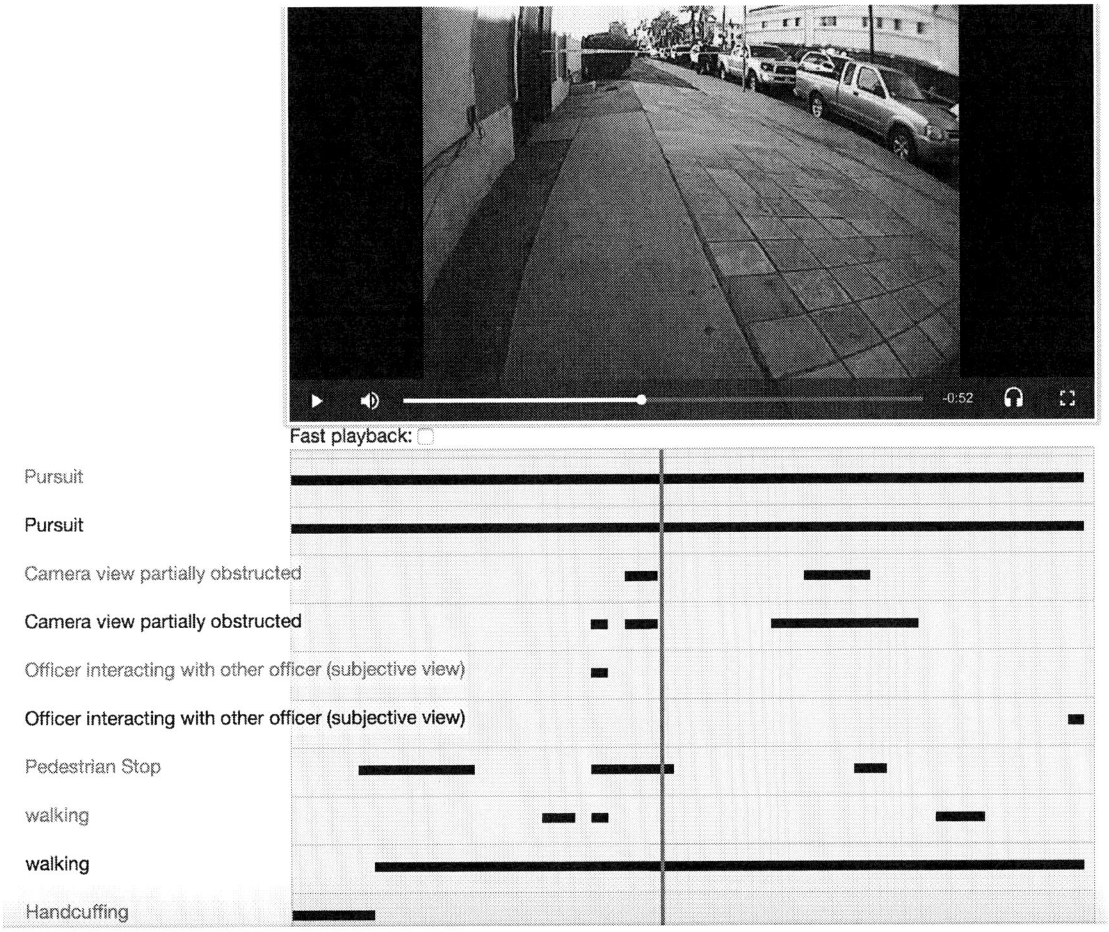

Figure 1: Illustration of the problem tackled in this paper with a timeline over a body worn camera video. Ground truth annotations are represented in black. Machine detected segments are represented in red. The neural network detect at the same time *Pedestrian Stop* and *Pursuit* which are disjoint activities.

This paper focus on modeling and then learning a class disjointness constraint. After giving class disjointness modeling examples related to our domain in Section 2 we formulate the constraint as a loss function applied on the disjoint classes. Then in Section 3 we conduct experiments on a synthetic dataset showing that this method effectively leads to an improvement in enforcing the constraint.

2 From an ontology axiom to a loss function

A long term goal of this work is to design a system where changes in the ontology would result in changes in the neural network training process. Especially we are interested in studying how modeling constraints as ontology axioms can result in adding specific losses on the neural network output classes corresponding to the ontology classes on which these axioms apply.

OWL2 (Motik et al., 2009) provides three constructs for expressing class disjointness. The main one `owl:disjointWith` is a class axiom specifying disjointness between this class and another. Multiple owl:disjointWith statements can be defined within a class description. In our use case, a set of topics are all disjoint for a given annotated video. OWL2 introduces a convenient way to model this using the owl:DisjointUnion construct allowing to specify the disjointness outside of the class definition. The statement below expresses that the class Topic has three disjoint subclasses Pedestrian Stop, Traffic Stop and Car Pursuit.[2]

```
owl:DisjointUnion(leo:Topic
                  leo:PedestrianStop
                  leo:TrafficStop
                  leo:CarPursuit)
```

Similarly we find it more convenient to express that two classes are disjoint in a separate axiom than in the classes definitions. The OWL2 construct `owl:DisjointClasses` allows to express that a set of classes is pairwise disjoint. The statement below expresses that an officer cannot be at the same time driving a car and be a the passenger of that car.

```
owl:DisjointClasses(leo:OfficerDriving
                    leo:OfficerPassenger)
```

With a large enough training data set, the constraints should be learnt by the model from the data. However, the dataset would need to cover all possible conditions that would happen when seeing new videos, and the space of possibilities is large. For example light conditions, vegetation, urban setting, police officers vehicles and uniforms can vary widely between police departments. There are multiple cases in other domains where the amount of data available for training may be limited, while the domain is quite complex. This can happen for reasons of data privacy, for example when dealing with personal or sensitive data, or when training happens on a user mobile device. Explicitly using ontological knowledge in the neural network training process will help the model avoiding to break these constraints on new data.

We propose here to study the effect of a specific objective function applied to the neural network outputs corresponding to the classes on the ontology for which a disjointness axiom was defined. This function should maximize loss when the constraint is broken, allowing only one class to be positively output. More specifically, in this paper we treat the case where one of the disjoint classes has to be selected by the network. A common objective function to achieve this is to use categorical cross-entropy (De Boer et al., 2005). This objective is usually used in combination with a Softmax activation. However, we do not want to modify the neural network architecture when introducing constraints, but only the objective function. We thus apply Softmax on the predictions before passing them to the objective function.

Equipped with this loss function for class disjointness we will next run experiments to study its influence on model training.

3 Experiments

Our experiments consist in testing the effect of the custom loss on forcing the neural network to learn the constraint. As motivated in the introduction of this paper, the sensitive character of the data we

[2]The leo namespace stands for Law Enforcement Ontology, an ongoing effort to model police officers interactions.

$$\begin{array}{r} \text{Disjoint classes} \begin{Bmatrix} 0.32543 & 0 \\ 0.93456 & 1 \\ 0.62334 & 0 \end{Bmatrix} \\ \text{Other classes} \begin{Bmatrix} 0.43655 & 0 \\ 0.92824 & 1 \\ 0.16593 & 0 \\ 0.61232 & 1 \end{Bmatrix} \end{array} \tag{1}$$

Figure 2: Example generated dataset. Input on the left columns are randomly generated. Output for disjoint classes is 1 for the highest value, 0 for the others. Output for the other classes is 1 if the input is greater than a threshold here set to 0.5, 0 otherwise.

are working with does not allow to share it for reproducibility. We thus present experiments on a synthetic dataset presented below. All the experiments and dataset generation code is open source and available at: `https://github.com/OpenAxon/constrained-nn`.

3.1 Dataset

In order to be able to control parameters of the dataset we work with and to speed up training experiments, we generate synthetic data using the following procedure. A number of pseudo-random numbers is generated for the input. Outputs are separated into two sets: one set that represents classes under the disjointness axiom and for which we would like the disjointness constraint to apply, and another set which represent the other classes. We set the number of outputs to be equal to the number of inputs and generate output values according to this: we take the argmax of the input set that represents disjoint classes, and assign the corresponding output to one. Every other output in the disjoint set is set to zero. The rest of the outputs are set to one if their corresponding input is greater than a given threshold, and to zero otherwise. Figure 1 illustrates inputs and corresponding output values.

In the context of these experiments we use a dataset with a hundred thousand data points, having 50 generic classes and 5 disjoint classes. We set the threshold parameter for generic classes to 0.5. We selected the number of generic classes and disjoint classes to be about the same size of the number of classes and disjoint classes we have in our law enforcement use case.

3.2 Model architecture

Our hypothesis is that adding the ontology constraint in the network as a specific loss function will help the network enforcing this constraint. We verify this by training and testing a model on the dataset presented above. The model architecture is detailed in Figure 3 below. It consists in a fully connected network with three layers having non-linear activations, and an output layer with a sigmoid activation. Each intermediate layers has 200 neurons. We use an Adam optimizer with a learning rate of 0.001.

We use this architecture to define two models by only changing the objective function: for the baseline we use binary cross-entropy on the whole set of output classes. For the constrained model we use a combination of binary cross-entropy defined on the non constrained classes, and the softmax categorical cross-entropy loss defined in Section 2 for the disjoint classes. A parameter controls the weight of the constraint loss with regards to the generic loss. We present our results below.

3.3 Results

Our goal is to compare how the model performs on learning the constraint for this dataset. In order to report this we define two metrics that measure how well the network can predict constrained and non-constrained classes correctly. Given P the set of predictions, G the ground truth and C the set of constrained classes, metrics are defined as follows:

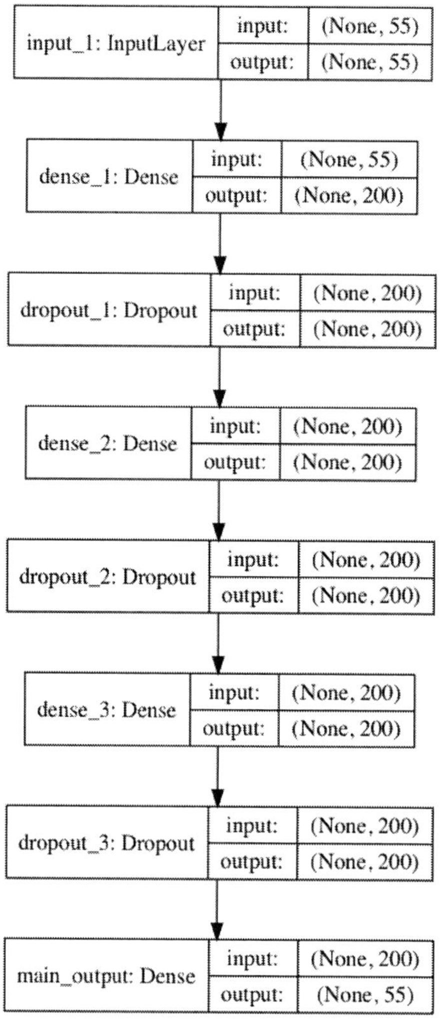

Figure 3: Model architecture. The None values are placeholders for the batch size.

- Constrained classes metrics: categorical classification accuracy

$$M_i = \frac{\sum_{c \in C}([P_i(c)] = G_i(c))}{|C|} \tag{2}$$

Where $[P_i(c)]$ represents the nearest integer to the prediction.

- Unconstrained classes metric: binary classification accuracy

$$M_i = (argmax_C(P_i) = argmax_C(G_i)) \tag{3}$$

for each batch b of the training set.

We perform multiple training runs using a batch size of 32 on three dataset with varying sizes. Reported numbers below are averaged for each batch. For each dataset we perform:

- one run for the baseline using a single loss.
- four runs for the constrained model using weights of 1, 2, 4 and 8 for on the constraint loss.

Three datasets are generated with size 5000, 10000 and 50000. Other dataset parameters are given in Section 3.1. Figures 4-6 below report results for the various configurations on each dataset.

As expected, overall accuracy increases as the datasets size increase. The weight on the constraint loss does not have a significant effect on the accuracy of the constrained outputs. However, as the weight increases, the accuracy on the unconstrained output decreases significantly. These observations are valid for the three datasets. As expected, the unconstrained model has difficulty learning

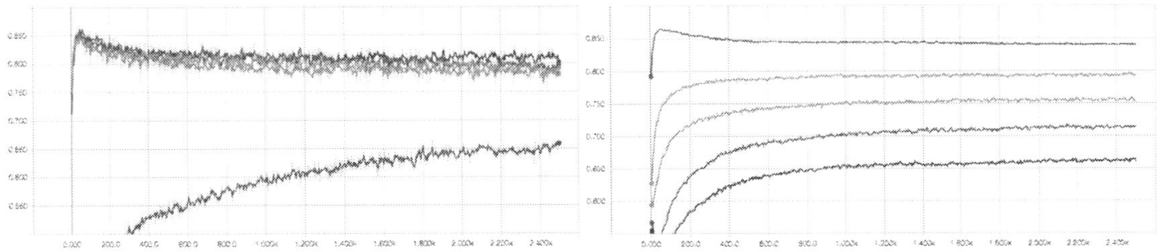

(a) Categorical classification validation accuracy on constrained outputs of the 5k dataset

(b) Binary classification validation accuracy on unconstrained outputs of the 5k dataset

Figure 4: Constraints on 5k dataset using various weights for the constraint loss.
Legend: green: no constraint, orange: w=1, cyan: w=2, magenta: w=4, blue: w=8

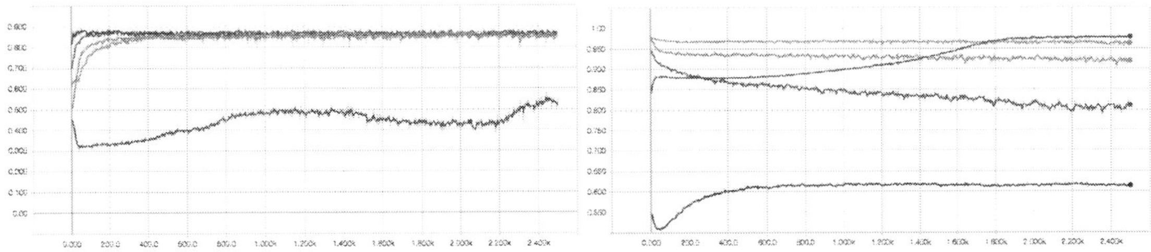

(a) Categorical classification validation accuracy on constrained outputs of the 10k dataset

(b) Binary classification validation accuracy on unconstrained outputs of the 10k dataset

Figure 5: Constraints on 10k dataset using various weights for the constraint loss
Legend: green: no constraint, orange: w=1, cyan: w=2, magenta: w=4, blue: w=8

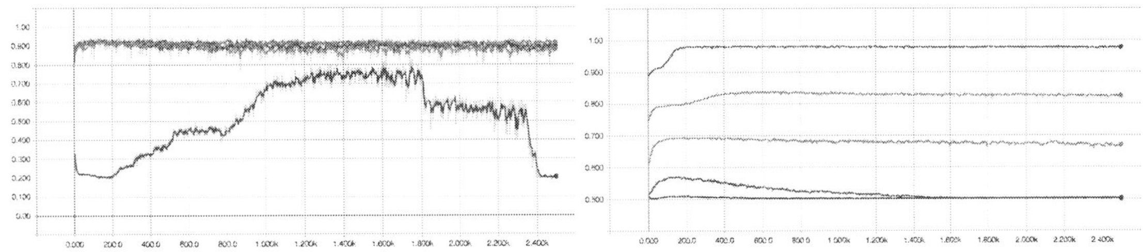

(a) Categorical classification validation accuracy on constrained outputs of the 50k dataset

(b) Binary classification validation accuracy on unconstrained outputs of the 50k dataset

Figure 6: Constraints on 50k dataset using various weights for the constraint loss
Legend: orange: no constraint, cyan: w=1, magenta: w=2, blue: w=4, green: w=8

the constraint on smaller datasets, but the gap between the models trained with a constrained loss and the model without the constrained loss decreases as the dataset size increases. This confirms the intuition than given enough data, explicit constraints might not be necessary. A constrained loss with a weight of 1 provides a very good tradeoff in loss of unconstrained accuracy versus improvement of the constrained outputs accuracy.

4 Related Work

Computer vision challenges provide unstructured or minimally structured labels, usually a list or a shallow taxonomy. Even fewer methods make use of the structure when it is provided.

The fast and accurate object detection system YOLO9000 (Redmon and Farhadi, 2016) makes use of the WordNet lexical database to build a hierarchy of concepts from the flat list of ImageNet labels. Predictions are then conditional probabilities of a concept class given its parent class. Prediction computation is performed by computing the softmax of all siblings at every level of the concept hierarchy. The predicted class is obtained by following the highest confidence path from the top of the concept hierarchy, until a threshold is reached. This approach is complementing our work and will likely be used in the system we are building.

In (Pathak et al., 2015) constraints are applied using a specific loss function in weakly supervised image segmentations. Only images labels are provided and constraints help the network identify images segments according to these labels. Constraints are defined specifying the presence or not of a class in the background or in the foreground according to the presence of a label. Another constraint specifies the relative number of pixels a class label is expected to occupy. The domain knowledge encoded in these constraints is specific to the datasets. It is possible to define the relative size of a class because the datasets contain iconic images where labels occupy a central position and a significant proportion of the image. The domain knowledge encoded in the constraints is thus dataset specific, rather than ontological. Our goal is to be able to transfer ontological knowledge of a domain that could apply to various datasets.

5 Conclusion

This work introduced constraints modeled in an ontology as part of a neural network training process. With these initial experiments we studied the usage of one class disjointness axiom over a set of classes. Adding the ontology axiom as a specific objective on the outputs corresponding to the disjoint classes provide a significant improvement: the classification accuracy of the network for the constraint is improved by 15 to 35 points depending on the dataset size. It is useful to note that adding the constrained loss does not result in a strict restriction, and the network may still in a few cases output classifications violating the constraint.

We plan to apply the class disjointness axioms in training models on actual video data. In order to be able to report on findings on these data, we are working toward building and releasing an open dataset of law enforcement videos, that we hope will help foster new research.

In future work we are interested to study the effect of multiple disjointness constraints. We are also studying how to model other ontology axioms as constraints. In a longer term, we are interesting in studying how ontology axioms can influence a neural network training process, but also how from an unconstrained neural network trained on a large dataset we could derive and materialize ontology axioms.

References

De Boer, P.-T., D. P. Kroese, S. Mannor, and R. Y. Rubinstein (2005). A tutorial on the cross-entropy method. *Annals of operations research 134*(1), 19–67.

Dean, M., G. Schreiber, S. Bechhofer, F. van Harmelen, J. Hendler, I. Horrocks, D. L. McGuinness, P. F. Patel-Schneider, and L. A. Stein (2004). OWL web ontology language reference. *W3C Recommendation February 10.*

Motik, B., P. F. Patel-Schneider, B. Parsia, C. Bock, A. Fokoue, P. Haase, R. Hoekstra, I. Horrocks, A. Ruttenberg, U. Sattler, and others (2009). OWL 2 web ontology language: Structural specification and functional-style syntax. *W3C recommendation 27*(65), 159.

Pathak, D., P. Krahenbuhl, and T. Darrell (2015). Constrained convolutional neural networks for weakly supervised segmentation. In *Proceedings of the IEEE International Conference on Computer Vision*, pp. 1796–1804.

Redmon, J. and A. Farhadi (2016, December). YOLO9000: Better, Faster, Stronger. *arXiv:1612.08242 [cs]*. arXiv: 1612.08242.

Russakovsky, O., J. Deng, H. Su, J. Krause, S. Satheesh, S. Ma, Z. Huang, A. Karpathy, A. Khosla, M. Bernstein, A. C. Berg, and L. Fei-Fei (2015, December). ImageNet Large Scale Visual Recognition Challenge. *International Journal of Computer Vision 115*(3), 211–252.

Full-Network Embedding in a Multimodal Embedding Pipeline

Armand Vilalta
Barcelona Supercomputing Center (BSC)
armand.vilalta@bsc.es

Dario Garcia-Gasulla
Barcelona Supercomputing Center (BSC)
dario.garcia@bsc.es

Ferran Parés
Barcelona Supercomputing Center (BSC)
ferran.pares@bsc.es

Jonatan Moreno
Barcelona Supercomputing Center (BSC)
jonatan.moreno@bsc.es

Eduard Ayguadé
Barcelona Supercomputing Center (BSC)
Universitat Politècnica de Catalunya
eduard.ayguade@bsc.es

Jesus Labarta
Barcelona Supercomputing Center (BSC)
Universitat Politècnica de Catalunya
jesus.labarta@bsc.es

Ulises Cortés
Barcelona Supercomputing Center (BSC)
Universitat Politècnica de Catalunya
ia@cs.upc.edu

Toyotaro Suzumura
Barcelona Supercomputing Center (BSC)
IBM T.J. Watson
tsuzumura@us.ibm.com

Abstract

The current state-of-the-art for image annotation and image retrieval tasks is obtained through deep neural networks, which combine an image representation and a text representation into a shared embedding space. In this paper we evaluate the impact of using the Full-Network embedding in this setting, replacing the original image representation in a competitive multimodal embedding generation scheme. Unlike the one-layer image embeddings typically used by most approaches, the Full-Network embedding provides a multi-scale representation of images, which results in richer characterizations. To measure the influence of the Full-Network embedding, we evaluate its performance on three different datasets, and compare the results with the original multimodal embedding generation scheme when using a one-layer image embedding, and with the rest of the state-of-the-art. Results for image annotation and image retrieval tasks indicate that the Full-Network embedding is consistently superior to the one-layer embedding. These results motivate the integration of the Full-Network embedding on any multimodal embedding generation scheme, something feasible thanks to the flexibility of the approach.

1 Introduction

Image annotation (also known as caption retrieval) is the task of automatically associating an input image with a describing text. Image annotation methods are an emerging technology, enabling semantic image indexing and search applications. The complementary task of associating an input text with a fitting image (known as image retrieval or image search) is also of relevance for the same sort of applications.

State-of-the-art image annotation methods are currently based on deep neural net representations, where an image embedding (*e.g.*, obtained from a convolutional neural network or CNN) and a text embedding (*e.g.*, obtained from a recurrent neural network or RNN) are combined into a unique multimodal embedding space. While several techniques for merging both spaces have been proposed [1, 2, 3, 4, 5, 6], little effort has been made in finding the most appropriate image embeddings to be used in that process. In fact, most approaches simply use a one-layer CNN embedding [7, 8]. In this paper we explore the impact of using a Full-Network embedding (FNE) [9] to generate the required image embedding, replacing the one-layer embedding. We do so by integrating the FNE into the multimodal embedding pipeline defined by Kiros et al. [1], which is based in the use of a Gated Recurrent Units neural network (GRU) [10] for text encoding and CNN for image encoding. Unlike one-layer embeddings, the FNE represents features of varying specificity in the context of the visual dataset, while also discretizes the features to regularize the space and alleviate the curse of dimensionality. These particularities result in a richer visual embedding space, which may be more reliably mapped to a common visual-textual embedding space.

The generic pipeline defined by Kiros et al. [1] has been recently outperformed in image annotation and image search tasks by methods specifically targeting one of those tasks [4, 11]. We choose to test our contribution on this pipeline for its overall competitive performance, expecting that any conclusion may generalize when applied to other solutions and tasks (*e.g.*, caption generation). This assumption would be dimmer if a more problem-specific methodology was chosen instead.

Our main goal is to establish the competitiveness of the FNE as an image representation to be used in caption related tasks. We test the suitability of this approach by evaluating its performance on both image annotation and image retrieval using three publicly available datasets: Flickr8k [12], Flickr30k [13] and MSCOCO [14]. Results obtained by the pipeline including the FNE are compared with the original pipeline of Kiros et al. [1] using a one-layer embedding, and also with the methods currently obtaining state-of-the-art results on the three datasets.

2 Related work

In the last few years, several solutions have been proposed to the problem of building common representations for images and text with the goal of enabling cross-domain search [1, 2, 3, 4, 5]. This paper builds upon the methodology described by Kiros et al. [1], which is in turn based on previous works in the area of Neural Machine Translation [15]. In their work, Kiros et al. [1] define a vectorized representation of an input text by using GRU RNNs. In this setting, each word in the text is codified into a vector using a word dictionary, vectors which are then fed one by one into the GRUs. Once the last word vector has been processed, the activations of the GRUs at the last time step conveys the representation of the whole input text in the multimodal embedding space. In parallel, images are processed through a Convolutional Neural Network (CNN) pre-trained on ImageNet [16], extracting the activations of the last fully connected layer to be used as a representation of the images. To solve the dimensionality matching between both representations (the output of the GRUs and the last fully-connected of the CNN) an affine transformation is applied on the image representation.

Similarly to the approach of Kiros et al. [1], most image annotation and image retrieval approaches rely on the use of CNN features for image representation. The current best overall performing model (considering both image annotation and image retrieval tasks) is the Fisher Vector (FV) [4], although its performance is most competitive on the image retrieval task. FV are computed with respect to the parameters of a Gaussian Mixture Model (GMM) and an Hybrid Gaussian-Laplacian Mixture Model (HGLMM). For both images and text, FV are build using deep neural network features; a VGG [17] CNN for images features, and a word2vec [18] for text features. For the specific problem of image annotation, the current state-of-art is obtained with the Word2VisualVec (W2VV) model [11]. This approach uses as a multimodal embedding space the same visual space where images are represented, involving a deeper text processing. Finally for the largest dataset we consider (MSCOCO), the best results in certain metrics are obtained by MatchCNN (m-CNN) [5], which is based on the use of CNNs to encode both image and text.

3 Methods

The multimodal embedding generator pipeline of Kiros et al. [1] represents images and textual captions in the same space. It is composed by two main elements, one which generates image embeddings and another one which generates text embeddings. We replace the original image embedding generator by

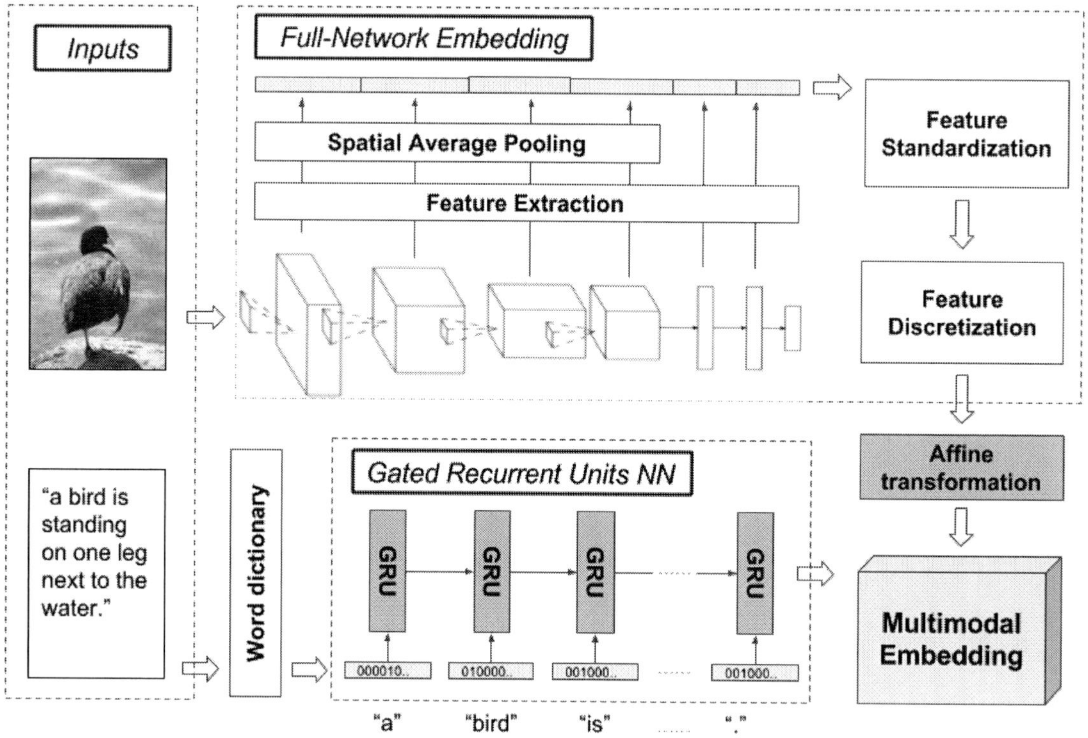

Figure 1: Overview of the proposed multimodal embedding generation pipeline with the integrated full-network embedding. Elements colored in orange are components modified during the neural network training phase. During testing, only one of the inputs is provided.

the FNE, which results in the architecture shown in Figure 1. Next we describe these components in further detail.

3.1 Full-network Embedding

The FNE generates a representation of an input image by processing it through a pre-trained CNN, and extracting the neural activations of all convolutional and fully-connected layers. After the initial feature extraction process, the FNE performs a dimensionality reduction step for convolutional activations, by applying a spatial average pooling on each convolutional filter. After the spatial pooling, every feature (from both convolutional and fully-connected layers) is standardized through the z-values, which are computed over the whole image train set. This standardization process puts the value of the each feature in the context of the dataset. At this point, the meaning of a single feature value is the degree with which the feature value is atypically high (if positive) or atypically low (if negative) in the context of the dataset. Zero marks the typical behavior.

The last step in the FNE pipeline is a feature discretitzation process. The previously standardized embedding is usually of large dimensionality (*e.g.*, 12,416 features for VGG16) which entails problems related with the curse of dimensionality. The usual approach to address this issue is to apply some dimensionality reduction methods (*e.g.*, PCA) [19, 20]. FNE uses a different approach, reducing expressiveness through the discretization of features, while keeping the dimensionality. Specifically, the FNE discretization maps the feature values to the $\{-1, 0, 1\}$ domain, where -1 indicates an unusually low value (*i.e.*, the feature is significant by its absence for an image in the context of the dataset), 0 indicates that the feature has an average value (*i.e.*, the feature is not significant) and 1 indicates an uncommonly high activation (*i.e.*, the feature is significant by its presence for an image in the context of the dataset). The mapping of standardized values into these three categories is done through the definition of two constant thresholds.

The optimal values of these thresholds can be found empirically for a labeled dataset [21]. Instead, we use threshold values shown to perform consistently across several domains [9].

3.2 Multimodal embedding

In our approach, we integrate the FNE with the multimodal embedding pipeline of Kiros et al. [1]. To do so we use the FNE to obtain an image representation instead of the output of the last layer of a CNN, as the original model does. The encoder architecture processing the text is used as it is, using a GRUs recurrent neural network to encode the sentences. To combine both embeddings, Kiros et al. [1] use an affine transformation on the image representation (in our case, the FNE) identical to a fully connected neural network layer. This extra layer is trained simultaneously with the GRUs. The elements of the multimodal pipeline that are tuned during the training phase of the model are shown in orange in Figure 1.

In simple terms, the training procedure consist on the optimization of the pairwise ranking loss between the correct image-caption pair and a random pair. Assuming that a correct pair of elements should be closer in the multimodal space than a random pair. The loss $\mathcal{L}$ can be formally defined as follows:

$$\mathcal{L} = \sum_{\mathbf{I}} \sum_{k} max\,\{0, \alpha - s(\mathbf{i}, \mathbf{c}) + s(\mathbf{i}, \mathbf{c}_k)\} + \sum_{\mathbf{C}} \sum_{k} max\,\{0, \alpha - s(\mathbf{i}, \mathbf{c}) + s(\mathbf{c}, \mathbf{i}_k)\} \tag{1}$$

Where $\mathbf{i}$ is an image vector, $\mathbf{c}$ is its correct caption vector, and $\mathbf{i}_k$ and $\mathbf{c}_k$ are sets of random images and captions respectively. The operator $s(\bullet, \bullet)$ defines the cosine similarity. This formulation includes a margin term α to avoid pulling the image and caption closer once their distance is smaller than the margin. This makes the optimization focus on distant pairs instead of improving the ones that are already close.

4 Experiments

In this section we evaluate the impact of using the FNE in a multimodal pipeline (FN-MME) for both image annotation and image retrieval tasks. To properly measure the relevance of the FNE, we compare the results of the FN-MME with those of the original multimodal pipeline reported by Kiros et al. [1] (CNN-MME). Additionally, we define a second baseline by using the original multimodal pipeline with a training configuration closer to the one used for the FNE experiments (*i.e.*, same source CNN, same MME dimensionality, *etc.*). We refer to this second baseline as CNN-MME*.

4.1 Datasets

In our experiments we use three different publicly available datasets:

The **Flickr8K** dataset [12] contains 8,000 hand-selected images from Flickr, depicting actions and events. Five correct captions are provided for each image. Following the provided splits, 6,000 images are used for train, 1,000 are used in validation and 1,000 more are kept for testing.

The **Flickr30K** dataset [13] is an extension of Flickr8K. It contains 31,783 photographs of everyday activities, events and scenes. Five correct captions are provided for each image. In our experiments 29,000 images are used for training, 1,014 conform the validation set and 1,000 are kept for test. These splits are the same ones used by Kiros et al. [1] and by Karpathy and Fei-Fei [22].

The **MSCOCO** dataset [14] includes images of everyday scenes containing common objects in their natural context. For captioning, 82,783 images and 413,915 captions are available for training, while 40,504 images and 202,520 captions are available for validation. Captions from the test set are not publicly available. Previous contributions consider using a subset of the validation set for validation and a different subset for test. In most cases, such subsets are composed by either 1,000 or 5,000 images for each set, with their corresponding 5 captions per image. In our experiments we consider both settings.

Table 1: Results obtained for the Flickr8 dataset. R@K is Recall@K (high is good). Med r is Median rank (low is good). Best results are shown in **bold**.

Model		Image Annotation				Image Retrieval			
		R@1	R@5	R@10	Med r	R@1	R@5	R@10	Med r
FV	[4]	21.2	50.0	64.8	5	**31.0**	**59.3**	**73.7**	**4**
m-CNN	[5]	24.8	53.7	67.1	5	20.3	47.6	61.7	5
Bi-LSTM	[24]	29.3	58.2	69.6	**3**	19.7	47.0	60.6	5
W2VV	[11]	**33.6**	**62.0**	**75.3**	**3**	-	-	-	-
CNN-MME	[1]	18.0	40.9	55.0	8	12.5	37.0	51.5	10
CNN-MME*		21.0	45.7	60.4	7	14.0	35.8	48.6	11
FN-MME		23.3	50.8	66.8	5	15.0	38.2	51.6	10

4.2 Implementation and Evaluation Details

The caption sentences are word-tokenized using the Natural Language Toolkit (NLTK) for Python [23]. The choice of the word embedding size and the number of GRUs has been analyzed to obtain a range of suitable parameters to test in the validation set. The total number of different words is 8,919 for Flickr8k, 22,962 for Flickr30k and 32,775 for MSCOCO. Using all the words present in the dataset is likely to produce overfitting problems when training on examples containing words that only occur a few times. This overfitting problem may not have a huge impact on performance, but it may add undesired noise in the multimodal representation. The original setup [1] limited the word embedding to the 300 most frequent words, while using 300 GRUs. The Bi-LSTM model [24] in contrast defines the vocabulary size to include words appearing more than 5 time in the dataset, leading to dictionaries of size 2,018 for Flickr8k, 7,400 for Flickr30k and 8,801 for MSCOCO. Our own preliminary experiments on the validation set showed that increasing multimodal space dimensionality and dictionary length slightly improved the performance of image retrieval, in detriment of image annotation. However, the combined performance difference remains rather small when using non-extreme parameter values (*e.g.*, a model with 10,000 words vocabulary on MSCOCO dataset show a 0.4% average recall reduction when compared with a 2,000 words model). Since we are building a model for solving both tasks, we kept the parameters obtaining the highest combined score in the validation set. For the Flickr datasets, the word embedding is limited to the 1,000 most frequent words. For the MSCOCO dataset, we use a larger dictionary, considering the 2,000 most frequent words. In both cases we use 2,048 GRUs, which is also the dimensionality of the resultant multimodal embedding space.

For generating the image embedding we use the classical VGG16 CNN architecture [17] as source model pretrained for ImageNet [16]. This architecture is composed of 16 convolutional layers combined with pooling layers followed by two fully connected layers and the final softmax output layer. When using the FNE, this results in a image embedding space of 12,416 dimensions.

On all our experiments (both the CNN-MME* and the FN-MME) the margin parameter α is set to 0.2, and the batch size to 128 image-caption pairs. Within the same batch, every possible alternative image-caption pair is used as contrasting example. The models are trained up to 25 epochs, and the best performing model on the validation set is chosen (*i.e.*, early stopping). We use gradient clipping for the GRUs with a threshold of 2. We use ADAM [25] as optimization algorithm, with a learning rate of 0.0002 for the Flickr datasets, and 0.00025 for MSCOCO.

To evaluate both image annotation and image retrieval we use the following metrics:

- **Recall@K** (R@K) is the fraction of images for which a correct caption is ranked within the top-K retrieved results (and vice-versa for sentences). Results are provided for R@1, R@5 and R@10.
- **Median rank** (Med r) of the highest ranked ground truth result.

Table 2: Results obtained for the Flickr30 dataset. R@K is Recall@K (high is good). Med r is Median rank (low is good). Best results are shown in **bold**.

Model		Image Annotation				Image Retrieval			
		R@1	R@5	R@10	Med r	R@1	R@5	R@10	Med r
FV	[4]	25.0	52.7	66.0	5	**35.0**	**62.0**	**73.8**	**3**
m-CNN	[5]	33.6	64.1	74.9	3	26.2	56.3	69.6	4
Bi-LSTM	[24]	28.1	53.1	64.2	4	19.6	43.8	55.8	7
W2VV	[11]	**39.7**	**67.0**	**76.7**	**2**	-	-	-	-
CNN-MME	[1]	23.0	50.7	62.9	5	16.8	42.0	56.5	8
CNN-MME*		30.4	58.0	69.5	4	18.9	44.6	57.0	7
FN-MME		30.4	61.8	73.2	3	22.1	47.6	59.8	6

Table 3: Results obtained for the MSCOCO dataset. Top part shows results when using 1,000 images as test set, while the bottom shows results when using 5,000 images for test. R@K is Recall@K (high is good). Med r is Median rank (low is good). Best results are shown in **bold**. † results not in original paper.

	Model		Image Annotation				Image Retrieval			
			R@1	R@5	R@10	Med r	R@1	R@5	R@10	Med r
test 1K	FV	[4]	25.1	59.8	76.6	4	**39.4**	67.9	80.9	**2**
	m-CNN	[5]	42.8	73.1	84.1	**2**	32.6	**68.6**	**82.8**	3
	CNN-MME †		43.4	75.7	**85.8**	**2**	31.0	66.7	79.9	3
	CNN-MME*		41.2	72.8	85.1	2	26.2	58.6	73.9	4
	FN-MME		**47.3**	**76.8**	**85.8**	**2**	31.4	65.4	78.7	3
test 5K	FV	[4]	10.8	28.3	40.1	17	**17.3**	**39.0**	**50.2**	**10**
	Bi-LSTM	[24]	16.6	39.4	52.4	9	11.6	30.9	43.4	13
	CNN-MME*		18.7	42.8	56.7	8	10.4	28.7	40.6	17
	FN-MME		**21.1**	**46.6**	**60.2**	**6**	13.4	34.6	47.4	12

4.3 Results

For both image annotation and image retrieval tasks on the Flickr8k dataset, Table 1 shows the results of the proposed FN-MME, the reported results of the original model CNN-MME, the results of the original model when using our configuration CNN-MME*, and the current state-of-the-art (SotA). Tables 2 and 3 are analogous for the Flickr30k and MSCOCO datasets. Additional results of the CNN-MME model were made publicly available later on by the original authors [26]. We include these for the MSCOCO dataset, which was not evaluated in the original paper [1].

First, let us consider the impact of using the FNE. On all cases, the multimodal pipeline proposed by Kiros et al. [1] obtains equal or better results when using the FNE. This is the case for the originally reported results (CNN-MME), for the results made available later on by the original authors (CNN-MME†), and for the experiments we do using same configuration as the FN-MME (CNN-MME*). The comparison we consider to be the most relevant is the FN-MME against the CNN-MME*, as these contain the least differences besides the image embedding being used. In this particular case, the FN-MME outperforms the CNN-MME* by 3 percentual points on average for the Flickr datasets, and roughly by 4 points for the MSCOCO dataset.

To measure the relevance of the improvement provided by using the FNE, we compare the FN-MME model with the current state-of-the-art for image annotation and image retrieval. For the Flickr datasets, particularly for image annotation tasks, the performance of the FN-MME is significantly closer to the state of the art than the other variants of the same model (CNN-MME, CNN-MME†, CNN-MME*). Remarkably, the FN-MME provides the best reported results on image annotation for the MSCOCO dataset. However, let us remark that the competitive W2VV method [11] has no reported results for MSCOCO. The results of the FN-MME for image retrieval tasks are significantly further from the state-of-the-art. Overall, the competitiveness of FN-MME increases with dataset size.

5 Conclusions

For the multimodal pipeline of Kiros et al. [1], using the Full-Network image embedding results in consistently higher performances than using a one-layer image embedding. These results suggest that the visual representation provided by the FNE is superior to the current standard for the construction of most multimodal embeddings.

When compared to the current state-of-the-art, the results obtained by the FN-MME are significantly less competitive than problem-specific methods. Since this happens for all models using the same pipeline (CNN-MME, CNN-MME†, CNN-MME*), these results indicate that the original architecture of Kiros et al. [1] is itself outperformed in general by more problem-specific techniques.

Since the FNE is compatible with most multimodal pipelines based on CNN embeddings, as future work of this paper we intend to evaluate the performance of the FNE when integrated into the current state-of-the-art on image annotation (W2VV [11]) and image retrieval (FV [4]). If the boost in performance obtained by the FNE on the Kiros et al. [1] pipeline translates to these other methods, such combination would be likely to define new state-of-the-art results on both tasks.

Acknowledgements

This work is partially supported by the Joint Study Agreement no. W156463 under the IBM/BSC Deep Learning Center agreement, by the Spanish Government through Programa Severo Ochoa (SEV-2015-0493), by the Spanish Ministry of Science and Technology through TIN2015-65316-P project, by the Generalitat de Catalunya (contracts 2014-SGR-1051), and by the Core Research for Evolutional Science and Technology (CREST) program of Japan Science and Technology Agency (JST).

References

[1] Ryan Kiros, Ruslan Salakhutdinov, and Richard S Zemel. Unifying visual-semantic embeddings with multimodal neural language models. *arXiv preprint arXiv:1411.2539*, 2014.

[2] Ryan Kiros, Ruslan Salakhutdinov, and Rich Zemel. Multimodal neural language models. In *Proceedings of the 31st International Conference on Machine Learning (ICML-14)*, pages 595–603, 2014.

[3] Andrej Karpathy, Armand Joulin, and Fei Fei F Li. Deep fragment embeddings for bidirectional image sentence mapping. In *Advances in neural information processing systems*, pages 1889–1897, 2014.

[4] Benjamin Klein, Guy Lev, Gil Sadeh, and Lior Wolf. Associating neural word embeddings with deep image representations using fisher vectors. In *Proceedings of the IEEE Conference on Computer Vision and Pattern Recognition*, pages 4437–4446, 2015.

[5] Lin Ma, Zhengdong Lu, Lifeng Shang, and Hang Li. Multimodal convolutional neural networks for matching image and sentence. In *Proceedings of the IEEE International Conference on Computer Vision*, pages 2623–2631, 2015.

[6] Qing Sun, Stefan Lee, and Dhruv Batra. Bidirectional beam search: Forward-backward inference in neural sequence models for fill-in-the-blank image captioning. *arXiv preprint arXiv:1705.08759*, 2017.

[7] Jeff Donahue, Yangqing Jia, Oriol Vinyals, Judy Hoffman, Ning Zhang, Eric Tzeng, and Trevor Darrell. Decaf: A deep convolutional activation feature for generic visual recognition. In *Icml*, volume 32, pages 647–655, 2014.

[8] Ali Sharif Razavian, Hossein Azizpour, Josephine Sullivan, and Stefan Carlsson. Cnn features off-the-shelf: an astounding baseline for recognition. In *Proceedings of the IEEE Conference on Computer Vision and Pattern Recognition Workshops*, pages 806–813, 2014.

[9] Dario Garcia-Gasulla, Armand Vilalta, Ferran Parés, Jonatan Moreno, Eduard Ayguadé, Jesus Labarta, Ulises Cortés, and Toyotaro Suzumura. An out-of-the-box full-network embedding for convolutional neural networks. *arXiv preprint arXiv:1705.07706*, 2017.

[10] Kyunghyun Cho, Bart Van Merriënboer, Dzmitry Bahdanau, and Yoshua Bengio. On the properties of neural machine translation: Encoder-decoder approaches. *arXiv preprint arXiv:1409.1259*, 2014.

[11] Jianfeng Dong, Xirong Li, and Cees GM Snoek. Word2visualvec: Image and video to sentence matching by visual feature prediction. *CoRR, abs/1604.06838*, 2016.

[12] Cyrus Rashtchian, Peter Young, Micah Hodosh, and Julia Hockenmaier. Collecting image annotations using amazon's mechanical turk. In *Proceedings of the NAACL HLT 2010 Workshop on Creating Speech and Language Data with Amazon's Mechanical Turk*, pages 139–147. Association for Computational Linguistics, 2010.

[13] Peter Young, Alice Lai, Micah Hodosh, and Julia Hockenmaier. From image descriptions to visual denotations: New similarity metrics for semantic inference over event descriptions. *Transactions of the Association for Computational Linguistics*, 2:67–78, 2014.

[14] Tsung-Yi Lin, Michael Maire, Serge Belongie, Lubomir Bourdev, Ross Girshick, James Hays, Pietro Perona, Deva Ramanan, C Lawrence Zitnick, and Piotr Dollar. Microsoft coco: Common objects in context. *arXiv preprint arXiv:1405.0312*, 2014.

[15] Ilya Sutskever, Oriol Vinyals, and Quoc V Le. Sequence to sequence learning with neural networks. In *Advances in neural information processing systems*, pages 3104–3112, 2014.

[16] Olga Russakovsky, Jia Deng, Hao Su, Jonathan Krause, Sanjeev Satheesh, Sean Ma, Zhiheng Huang, Andrej Karpathy, Aditya Khosla, Michael Bernstein, et al. Imagenet large scale visual recognition challenge. *International Journal of Computer Vision*, 115(3):211–252, 2015.

[17] Karen Simonyan and Andrew Zisserman. Very deep convolutional networks for large-scale image recognition. *arXiv preprint arXiv:1409.1556*, 2014.

[18] Tomas Mikolov, Ilya Sutskever, Kai Chen, Greg S Corrado, and Jeff Dean. Distributed representations of words and phrases and their compositionality. In *Advances in neural information processing systems*, pages 3111–3119, 2013.

[19] Arsalan Mousavian and Jana Kosecka. Deep convolutional features for image based retrieval and scene categorization. *arXiv preprint arXiv:1509.06033*, 2015.

[20] Hossein Azizpour, Ali Sharif Razavian, Josephine Sullivan, Atsuto Maki, and Stefan Carlsson. Factors of transferability for a generic convnet representation. *IEEE Transactions on Pattern Analysis and Machine Intelligence*, 38(9):1790–1802, 2016.

[21] Dario Garcia-Gasulla, Ferran Parés, Armand Vilalta, Jonatan Moreno, Eduard Ayguadé, Jesús Labarta, Ulises Cortés, and Toyotaro Suzumura. On the behavior of convolutional nets for feature extraction. *arXiv preprint arXiv:1703.01127*, 2017.

[22] Andrej Karpathy and Li Fei-Fei. Deep visual-semantic alignments for generating image descriptions. In *Proceedings of the IEEE Conference on Computer Vision and Pattern Recognition*, pages 3128–3137, 2015.

[23] Steven Bird. Nltk: the natural language toolkit. In *Proceedings of the COLING/ACL on Interactive presentation sessions*, pages 69–72. Association for Computational Linguistics, 2006.

[24] Cheng Wang, Haojin Yang, Christian Bartz, and Christoph Meinel. Image captioning with deep bidirectional lstms. In *Proceedings of the 2016 ACM on Multimedia Conference*, pages 988–997. ACM, 2016.

[25] Diederik Kingma and Jimmy Ba. Adam: A method for stochastic optimization. *arXiv preprint arXiv:1412.6980*, 2014.

[26] Ryan Kiros. visual-semantic-embedding. URL `https://github.com/ryankiros/visual-semantic-embedding`.

Extracting tags from large raw texts using End-to-End memory networks

Feras Al Kassar
LIRIS lab - UCBL Lyon1
en.feras@hotmail.com

Frédéric Armetta
LIRIS lab - UCBL Lyon1
frederic.armetta@liris.cnrs.fr

17-07-2017

Abstract

Recently, new approaches based on Deep Learning have demonstrated good capacities to manage Natural Language Processing problems. In this paper, after selecting End-to-End Memory Networks for its ability to efficiently capture context meanings, we study its behavior when facing large semantic problems (large texts, large vocabulary sets) and apply it to automatically extract tags from a website. A new data set is proposed, results and parameters are discussed. We show that the so formed system can capture the correct tags most of the time, and can be an efficient and advantageous way to complement other approaches because of its ability for generalization and semantic abstraction.

1 Introduction

To automatically extract the meaning of a web page or a raw text is still a deep challenge. Rule-based approaches which have been applied for years are efficient but can't manage easily diversity, and suffer from hand-made drawbacks like the difficulty to model a rich word built of complex interacting semantical concepts. Natural Language Processing (NLP) based on Deep Learning have recently been applied to capture the meaning of texts, and to build inferences so that it could be possible, as a long term goal, to have a full and natural discussion with such a system (Li et al. (2016)).

In this paper, after covering some of the deep learning methods to address NLP problem's, we select a promising *End-to-End Memory Networks* approach for its ability to capture the meaning of complex words associations. As presented in section 2, this approach has been designed to preserve the memory of texts acquired.

For our study, we apply the approach to a large problem, so that we can see how the *End-to-End Memory Networks* can be applied to the Web. We choose to study long texts (biographies), with a large set of words leading to a high memory and computing consumption. The section 4 introduces and motivates the elaboration of a new dataset based on biographies proposed by the website `http://biography.com`. Experimental results and parameters are then discussed in section 5. Section 6 concludes and introduces some perspectives.

2 State of the art and positioning

Capturing the meaning of texts requires to capture the meaning of words, and the meaning of word associations. Words can be efficiently represented by a dedicated embedding. World associations can be captured considering their sequentiality.

Recurrent neural networks (RNN), can be applied to capture the order between words. In this case, the network is progressively fed, word after word. The network tends to forget long relation between words for large texts. Long Short Term Memories (LSTM, Hochreiter and Schmidhuber (1997)) allows to moderate this limitation. On their side, Memory Networks can be fed by an aggregation of words in one step. Based a some state of the art comparison results, we can discuss the ways to address the problem, and settle on Memory Networks for their ability to manage efficiently word embeddings and complex semantic contexts.

2.1 Word embeddings

The word embeddings aim to find a representation for strings in a high dimensional space. The general idea is to learn appropriate vectors for each of the available words as presented in Mikolov et al. (2013). Doing so, a distributed representation for words in a vectorial space manifests good properties as a base to learn the languages: similar words will be placed close to each other. The learning is really rich, it will not just be about the semantic (equation 1) but it will also be about syntactic (equation 2).

$$Vec(\text{“}Italy\text{”}) + Vec(\text{“}Rome\text{”}) - Vec(\text{“}France\text{”}) = Vec(\text{“}Paris\text{”}) \tag{1}$$

$$Vec(\text{“}run\text{”}) + Vec(\text{“}running\text{”}) - Vec(\text{“}walk\text{”}) = Vec(\text{“}walking\text{”}) \tag{2}$$

The computational and memory consumption for embeddings highly rely on the size of the dictionary. It is possible to limit the number of the words in the vocabulary. In this way we reduce the size of the network and reach better computational results. So for example the repetition words like “a”, “an” or “the” will not provide a valuable information to understand the sentence and can be removed. We can apply a filter applying the following probability to discard the meaningless words, where the function f stands for the frequency of the word.

$$P(W_i) = 1 - \sqrt{\frac{t}{f(W_t)}} \tag{3}$$

Starting from a word embedding, one can then complete the approach to capture the meaning of the sentences or complete texts.

2.2 RNN and LSTM

Recurrent Neural Networks (RNN) contain loops that allow to feed the network step-by-step (word-by-word for an NLP problem). Nevertheless, long-term dependencies are not well supported because of the gradient vanishing problem (Pascanu et al. (2012)). LSTM (Long Short Term Memory) partially solved this problem by using a forgetting factor. They allow to protect data to remember, and allow to forget the useless ones.

2.3 Memory Networks and End-to-End Memory Networks

One other way to consider memory for sentences is to agglomerate sentences directly in selected slots. This is what has been proposed in Weston et al. (2014). The first Memory Networks proposal requires a layer-by-layer learning. An extension of this work called *End-to-End memory networks* allows a full back propagation for the network with no additional costs as presented in Sukhbaatar et al. (2015).

The general idea relies on imitating the human brain memory. The human memory retrieves some data from its memory thanks to global contexts completed by stimuli or events. End-to-End memory networks follow the same idea, i.e., when we write the current experience (a story) inside the memory followed by an event (a query), the appropriated knowledge is propagated to the end of the memory network thanks to the neural network well-known ability to generalize past experiences.

2.4 Comparative results

Lets consider the experiments proposed in Hill et al. (2015) and and Weston et al. (2015) which propose answering question models experimented on short stories. The first one was about using the question-answer formulation while focusing on predicting the missing word inside the question. The dataset was formed by some children books shaped sequentially using the following pattern: 20 sentences were used as a story, the next sentence was altered (one word was removed) and used as a question and so on.

The size of the vocabulary set is about 53.000, with a fixed number of sentences inside the memory (20 sentences). We can see comparative results, somehow equivalent, between LSTM and End to End memory network in table 1.

Table 1: Children's Books experiments, Hill et al. (2015)

LSTM	65%
End-to-End Memory Network	67%

For the second experiments proposed in Weston et al. (2015), stories involve rooms, people and objects. The query refers to the places of the objects. For this problem, the semantic acquisition has to be refined in order to apply inferences and deduce the position for objects. This dataset manipulates a small number of words (around 20 words), the size of the sentences is also limited (7 words and small story containing less than 20 sentences). We can see comparative between LSTM and Memory Network in table 2.

Table 2: Toy Tasks experiments, Weston et al. (2015)

LSTM	49%
Memory Network	93%

We can notice that the End-to-End memory networks are working better to extract the meaning of specific objects than predicting words. That is why we choose to experiment and test this approach for automatic extraction of tags. In order to study the scale sensibility for the approach, we will focus on a larger vocabulary set size with a larger amount of sentences standing for the context to capture.

3 End-to-End Memory Networks description

In this section, we will detail the one layer inference mechanism of end-to-end memory networks. The global approach allows to cover the network more than one time to compute complex inferences but is not used nor detailed here. Indeed, for the tag capturing problem, additional layers hasn't provided any significant gain in our experiments (see Sukhbaatar et al. (2015) for a complete description of the approach), the context can be captured with only one covering of the network.

The model aims to define continuous representations for each sentences in the stories and for the queries, then this representation is processed to generate at the output the answer of the query, as presented in figure 1. The learning is supervised and will propagate the error back through the network in order to apply network weights corrections.

3.1 Sentence representation

The memory relies in slots for each of the sentences of the story $x_1, x_2, ..., x_n$. Every x_i will be converted to a memory vector m_i of dimension d computed by embedding each x_i in a continuous space using an embedding matrix A (of size $d \times V$, with V set as the size of the dictionary). In the same manner, the query q will be embedded by a matrix B with the same dimensions to obtain the internal state u.

The temporal context for sentences is really important to catch. Each sentence is represented by the sum of pondered word embeddings: m_i will be $m_i = \sum_j l_j.Ax_{ij}$ where l_j is a column vector with the structure $l_{kj} = (1 - j/J) - (k/d)(1 - 2j/J)$ with J being the number of words in the sentence, and d the dimension of the embedding. The same representation is used for questions, memory inputs and memory outputs.

An other more precise way to refine the sentence contexts stands on modifying the memory vector $m_i = \sum_j Ax_{ij} + T_A(i)$ where the ith row of a special matrix T_A encodes temporal information. And in the same way $c_i = \sum_j Cx_{ij} + T_C(i)$. Both T_A and T_C are learned during training.

3.2 Propagation of the meaning through the network

We can compute the matching between u and every memory m_i by taking the *softmax* of the inner product, as described by equation 4.

$$P_i = Softmax(u^T m_i) \tag{4}$$

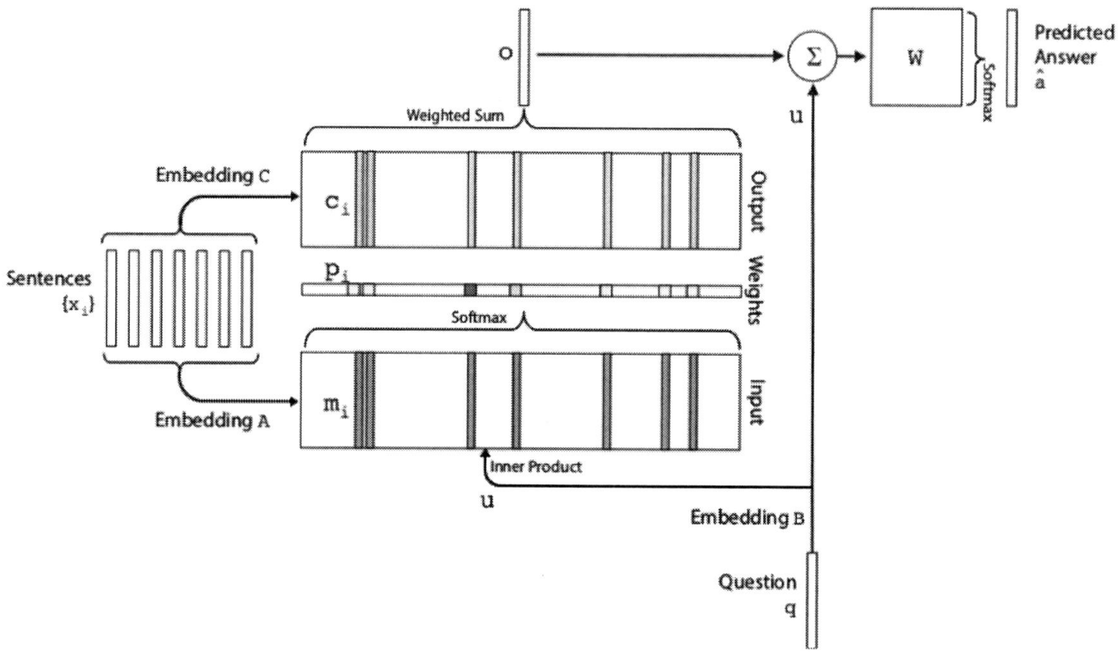

Figure 1: First part of the End to End Memory Network extracted from Sukhbaatar et al. (2015)

After that every inputs x_i will be embedded by an other matrix C with the same dimensions of A and B, then it will produce c_i for every input. The output o is the sum over the transformed inputs c_i weighted by the probability vector from the input, as presented in equation 5.

$$o = \sum_i P_i C_i \tag{5}$$

One can understand that the embeddings A and B are tuned for question-sentence correlation, while the embedding C is used to extract the meaning from previously selected relevant sentences from the story or context.

At the end, to generate the final prediction, we apply a *softmax* function to the sum of the output vector o with the question embedding u then passed through a final weight matrix W of size $V \times d$ (see equation 6).

$$\hat{a} = Softmax(W(o + u)) \tag{6}$$

4 Selected data set

4.1 Biography.com

Biography is a website containing over 7.000 profiles for famous people in many domains like Politics, Cinema, History, Sport, etc. The information provided by the website is daily updated and every person profile has a picture, tags and a raw text formed by titled paragraphs. As an example, the figure 2 shows the first part of the profile of Victor Hugo, a famous French author.

The supervision for the learning has been possible thanks to the tags extracted from the website. To do so, we automatically generate a question, like What is Victor Hugos occupation? (for each person), we educate the network so that it can infer the good answer and capture the relevant parts of the raw text.

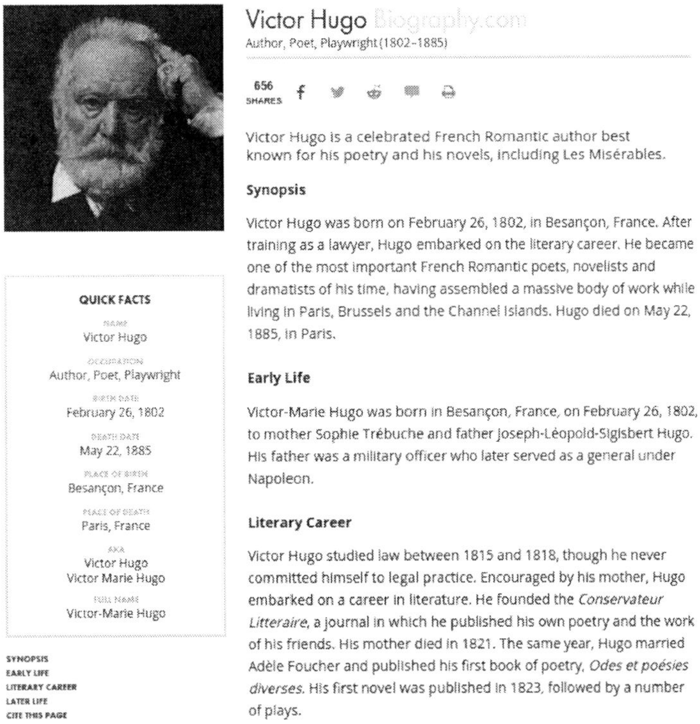

Figure 2: Victor Hugo profile in Biography.com

4.2 Extracting and Preparing the data

To extract the data from the website we used python with Selenium library to simulate a browser, this allows to request every article and extract the article with the tags. We extracted 6000 profiles. We then divided the articles into sentences using NLTK library in python and we deleted the repeated words. The longest article has 410 sentences, the average of the provided sentences is 49. The vocabulary size is 54.928 and the longest sentence has 88 words.

4.3 Hardware

We used a strong graphic card (NVIDIA TITAN X where GPU Architecture: Pascal, Frame buffer: 12 GB G5X, Memory Speed: 10 Gbps,Boost Clock Actual: 1531 MHz) to make the Tensorflow (specific machine/deep learning library which allows GPU computing) processing as efficient as possible.

We use 4500 profiles for the training with one question for every profile and 1500 profiles for testing. The training took about half an hour for each of our experiments.

5 Experimental results

The goal of this implementation is to test the limits of the end-to-end memory network and apply it on a complex and large data set extracted from a website, observing the results and evaluating the difficulties to reach the best solution. This algorithm needs to tune many parameters (the memory size, the embedding dimensions and the number of epochs).

We tried two strategies to deal with the parameters: the first one was to vary values for the memory size, the number of epochs and the embedding dimensions. The memory loads be the whole story, so each time the story is longer than the memory the model only keep the last sentences. We used 4500 profiles for the training with one question for every profile and 1500 profiles for the testing (table 3 and table 4).

Next we studied the influence of the embedding dimensions. Increasing the embedding dimensions and memory size causes the program to run out of memory. We can notice also that increasing

Table 3: Result 1

Epochs	Embedding Dimensions	Memory Size	Result
20	50	10	0.545
20	50	50	0.62
20	50	100	0.635
20	50	150	0.59
20	50	200	**0.65**
20	50	250	0.61
20	50	300	0.625
20	50	350	0.615
20	50	400	0.64

Table 4: Result 2

Epochs	Embedding Dimensions	Memory Size	Result
40	50	10	0.56
40	50	50	0.62
40	50	100	0.65
40	50	150	**0.655**
40	50	200	0.63
40	50	250	0.605
40	50	300	0.63
40	50	350	0.62
40	50	400	0.60

the embedding size will not enhance the results quality, when the best result in this testing was with embedding dimensions 100 and memory size 100 with a mean result of 0.685/1 information retrieving.

In order to check the validity of our hyper-parameters, we applied genetic algorithms (Mitchell (1998)). The best result was 0.665 with the embedding dimensions set to 144, the memory size set to 86 and 20 epochs. The parameters for the genetic algorithm was a population size of 35, 10 generations, the embedding dimensions allowed was set between 10 and 450 and the memory size allowed between 10 and 400.

We can compare our results with the children's books presented in section 2.4, even if it is not the same problem: our work is about extracting information from the a raw text from a long story (the longest story has 410 sentences) with unrestricted sentences size (the longest sentence has 88 words), while the children's books focus on predicting the words with short story 20 sentences. Nevertheless, both of them are using a large vocabulary size (around 50.000) and use End-to-End memory networks (table 7).

To have a semantic deep view of the results, let us see some of the predictions. For example: Rielle Hunter has no occupation for her in the biography but the model predicted her as a queen, with deep looking we can see she is married with John Edwards whose occupation was an U.S. representative. So the system probably exploited the relation between them, inferring on the way to defined her relation with her husband.

Table 5: Result 3

Epochs	Embedding Dimensions	Memory Size	Result
20	100	50	0.64
20	100	100	**0.685**
20	100	150	0.65
20	100	200	0.645
20	100	250	ME

Table 6: Result 4

Epochs	Embedding Dimensions	Memory Size	Result
20	150	50	0.665
20	150	100	0.66
20	150	150	ME

Table 7: Children's books and Biography profiles

	The goal	Memory Size	Embedding Dimensions	Vocabulries	Results
Children's Book	Predict the missing word	20	N.C.	53.000	65%
Biography profiles	Extract the occupation	100	100	54.000	68%

6 Conclusion and perspectives

In this work, we are interested in studying deep learning abilities to capture semantic inferred tags from a website. Our motivation is first to identify an approach able to learn large contexts or texts, while using large set of vocabularies. We show that memory networks manifest good properties for this kind of problems. Our results show that, for the selected tag retrieving problem, the system doesn't suffer so much from the large problems we tackle and associated memory sizes. It can succeed in identifying relevant parts of large texts used by its inference process for more than 65% of the cases. Some keywords express close meanings (poet, author, writer, etc.) and because the system is looking for an exact matching, probably success should be at a slighter higher score that what is reported here. Nevertheless, these results are already really encouraging and can be really useful to complement a rule based approach or other statistical approaches. The application of the network to a webpage is really quick, so that we can envisage for further works to apply the network for enhanced queries on the web. Many applications can be considered to make benefits from this new tool for natural language processing (social comments meaning extraction, product recommendation, etc.).

Acknowledgements

We gratefully acknowledge the support of NVIDIA Corporation with the donation of the Titan X Pascal GPU used for this research. This project is the result of a cooperation between the LIRIS laboratory and the Deal On company (`http://www.dealon.fr`).

References

Hill, F., A. Bordes, S. Chopra, and J. Weston (2015). The goldilocks principle: Reading children's books with explicit memory representations. *CoRR abs/1511.02301*.

Hochreiter, S. and J. Schmidhuber (1997, November). Long short-term memory. *Neural Comput. 9*(9), 1735–1780.

Li, J., A. H. Miller, S. Chopra, M. Ranzato, and J. Weston (2016). Dialogue learning with human-in-the-loop. *CoRR abs/1611.09823*.

Mikolov, T., I. Sutskever, K. Chen, G. S. Corrado, and J. Dean (2013). Distributed representations of words and phrases and their compositionality. In C. J. C. Burges, L. Bottou, M. Welling, Z. Ghahramani, and K. Q. Weinberger (Eds.), *Advances in Neural Information Processing Systems 26*, pp. 3111–3119. Curran Associates, Inc.

Mitchell, M. (1998). *An Introduction to Genetic Algorithms*. Cambridge, MA, USA: MIT Press.

Pascanu, R., T. Mikolov, and Y. Bengio (2012). Understanding the exploding gradient problem. *CoRR abs/1211.5063*.

Sukhbaatar, S., A. Szlam, J. Weston, and R. Fergus (2015). End-to-end memory networks. In *Proceedings of the 28th International Conference on Neural Information Processing Systems*, NIPS'15, Cambridge, MA, USA, pp. 2440–2448. MIT Press.

Weston, J., A. Bordes, S. Chopra, and T. Mikolov (2015). Towards ai-complete question answering: A set of prerequisite toy tasks. *CoRR abs/1502.05698.*

Weston, J., S. Chopra, and A. Bordes (2014). Memory networks. *CoRR abs/1410.3916.*

Dealing with Co-reference in Neural Semantic Parsing

Rik van Noord
CLCG, University of Groningen
r.i.k.van.noord@rug.nl

Johan Bos
CLCG, University of Groningen
johan.bos@rug.nl

Abstract

Linguistic phenomena like pronouns, control constructions, or co-reference give rise to co-indexed variables in meaning representations. We review three different methods for dealing with co-indexed variables in the output of neural semantic parsing of abstract meaning representations: (a) copying concepts during training and restoring co-indexation in a post-processing step; (b) explicit indexing of co-indexation; and (c) using absolute paths to designate co-indexing. The second method gives the best results and outperforms the baseline by 2.9 F-score points.

1 Introduction

Semantic parsing is the task of mapping a natural language sentence into a meaning representation (a logical form). One of the problems a semantic parser has to deal with is co-indexed variables, which arise in antecedent-anaphor relations, proper name co-reference, control constructions and other linguistic phenomena. Examples of such constructions are given in (1)–(4):

(1) Bob_i likes himself_i.
(2) Jack_i wants ϵ_i to buy an ice-cream.
(3) Peter_i sold his_i car.
(4) Sue_i saw Mary_j, but Mary_j did not see Sue_i.

In the context of this paper, we represent meanings using the formalism of Abstract Meaning Representation (AMR), as introduced by Banarescu et al. (2013). AMRs can be seen as graphs connecting concepts by relations. Each concept is represented by a named instance. Co-reference is established by re-using these instances. For example, the AMRs corresponding to examples (1) and (2) above are given in Figure 1. Note that, due to the bracketing, the variable *b* encapsulates the whole entity `person :name "Bob"` and not just `person`, i.e. *b* stands for a person with the name Bob.

```
(l / like-01
   :ARG0 (b / person :name "Bob")
   :ARG1 b)
```

```
(w / want-01
   :ARG1 (p / person :name "Jack")
   :ARG3 (b / buy-01
            :ARG1 p
            :ARG2 (i / ice-cream)))
```

Figure 1: AMRs representing the meaning of examples (1) and (2).

That there is a lot to gain in this area can be seen by applying the AMR evaluation suite of Damonte et al. (2017), which calculates nine different metrics to evaluate AMR parsing, *reentrancy* being one of them. Out of the four systems that made these scores available (all scores reported in van Noord and Bos (2017)), the reentrancy metric obtained the lowest F-score for three of them.

Various methods have been proposed to automatically parse AMRs, ranging from syntax-based approaches (e.g. Flanigan et al. (2014); Wang et al. (2015); Pust et al. (2015); Damonte et al. (2017)) to the more recent neural approaches (Peng et al. (2017); Buys and Blunsom (2017); Konstas et al. (2017); Foland and Martin (2017); van Noord and Bos (2017)). Especially the neural approaches are interesting, since they all use some sort of linearization method and therefore need a predefined way to handle reentrancy. Peng et al. (2017) and Buys and Blunsom (2017) use a special character to indicate reentrancy and restore co-referring variables in a post-processing step. Konstas et al. (2017) simply replace reentrancy variables by their co-referring concept in the input and never outputs co-referring nodes. Foland and Martin (2017) and van Noord and Bos (2017) use the same input transformation as Konstas et al. (2017), but do try to restore co-referring nodes by merging all equal concepts into a single concept in a post-processing step. All these methods have in common that they are not very sophisticated, but more importantly, that it is not clear what the exact impact of these methods is on the final performance of the model, making it unclear what the best implementation is for future neural AMR parsers.

In this paper we present three methods to handle reentrancy for AMR parsing. The first two methods are based on the previous work described above, while the third is a new, more principled method. These methods are applied on the model that reported the best results in the literature, the character-level neural semantic parsing method of van Noord and Bos (2017). In a nutshell, this method uses a character-based sequence-to-sequence model to translate sentences to AMRs. To enable this process, pre-processing and post-processing steps are needed. The aim of this paper is to find the best method to handle reentrancy in neural semantic parsing and to show the specific impact that each of the methods have on general performance.

2 Abstract Meaning Representations

AMRs, as introduced by Banarescu et al. (2013), are acyclic, directed graphs that show a representation of the meaning of a sentence. There are three ways to display an AMR: as a graph, as a tree, or as a set of triples. The AMRs in Figure 1 are shown as trees, which is also the input for our neural semantic parser. AMR concepts (e.g. like, person) are relating to each other by the use of two-place predicates (e.g. `:ARG0`, `:ARG1`, `:name`). For example, in the right AMR in Figure 1, *want* and *buy* are connected by the `:ARG3` predicate.

For our experiments, we use the annotated AMR corpus LDC2016E25, which contains 36,521 training, 1,368 development and 1,371 test AMRs. Co-indexed variables occur frequently in this data set, as can be seen in Table 1. About half of the AMRs contain at least one co-indexed variable, while about 20% of the total number of triples[1] contains a variable that has at least one anaphor in the AMR. This is the number of triples that is used in the reentrancy evaluation metric by Damonte et al. (2017). This number, however, also includes triples that would be present regardless of whether the variable is co-indexed (e.g. the instance triple of the antecedent). A more fair number might be the relation triples that contain an anaphor variable, which is exactly equal to the number of total co-indexed variables. This is still 3.4 to 4.2% of all triples in the data set.

Table 1: Statistics about the co-indexed variables in the AMR data set.

	Num AMRs	Num AMRs with reentrancy	Total number of reentrancies	Total triples	Triples containing co-indexed var
Training	36,520	17,589	40,582	968,512	189,426
Dev	1,368	706	1,590	46,737	8,704
Test	1,371	749	2,033	48,252	9,686
Silver	100,00	16,235	18,865	3,001,169	109,676

[1]Triples are used to evaluate AMR parsing systems, and are explained in Cai and Knight (2013).

3 Method

3.1 Variable-free AMRs

The actual values of the variables for AMR instances are unimportant. Hence, one can rename variables in an AMR as long as re-occurrences of variables are preserved. If variables are used only once in an AMR, they can therefore be completely eliminated from an AMR. This insight was used by Barzdins and Gosko (2016) in the first approach to neural semantic parsing of AMRs, because particular names of variables are very hard to learn for a neural model given the limited amount of data available. We present three ways to encode co-reference in variable-free AMRs.[2]

Method 1A: Baseline Note that if there are co-indexed variables, there is always exactly one instance of the variable that carries semantic information. In our baseline method, similar to Barzdins and Gosko (2016) and Konstas et al. (2017), we simply copy this semantic information, while removing the variables, as is shown below. This method does never output reentrancy nodes and therefore functions as a baseline. An example is shown in Figure 2.

```
(like-01
    :ARG0 (person :name "Bob")
    :ARG1 (person :name "Bob"))
```

```
(want-01
    :ARG1 (person :name "Jack")
    :ARG3 (buy-01
          :ARG1 (person :name "Jack")
          :ARG2 (ice-cream)))
```

Figure 2: Baseline representations of examples (1) and (2).

Method 1B: Reentrancy Restoring This method is created to restore reentrancy nodes in the output of the baseline model. It operates on a very ad hoc principle: if two nodes have the same concept, the second one was actually a reference to the first one. We therefore replace each node that has already occurred in the AMR by the variable of the antecedent node. This approach was applied by van Noord and Bos (2017) and Foland and Martin (2017).

The model thus never *learns* to output reentrancy, but the co-indexed variables are restored in a post-processing step. An example is shown in Figure 3. Note that this process can also erroneously insert reentrancies when two separate entities would be correct. For example, if the sentence *Bob*$_i$ *likes Bob*$_j$ refers to two different Bobs, the initial AMR in Figure 3 would have been correct.

```
(l / like-01
  :ARG0 (p / person :name "Bob")
  :ARG1 (p2 / person :name "Bob"))
```

```
(l / like-01
  :ARG0 (p / person :name "Bob")
  :ARG1 p)
```

Figure 3: Example of the Reentrancy Restoring method for example (1). Initial AMR on the left, reentrancy restored AMR on the right.

Method 2: Indexing This method comprises of removing all variables from an AMR, except when they are co-indexed. The remaining variables are normalised by converting them to numbers, so that each unique co-indexed variable has a unique identifier. Similar approaches were applied by Peng et al. (2017) and Buys and Blunsom (2017), and an example is shown in Figure 4. In this approach the model actually learns where it should output reentrancy nodes, instead of restoring them in a post-processing step.

However, we do still need some post-processing, as is shown in Figure 5 (after variables are restored). In this AMR, there is an index that is never instantiated (`*3*`) and an instantiated index that is never

[2]All pre- and post-processing scripts are available at https://github.com/RikVN/AMR.

```
(like-01                                    (want-01
  :ARG0 (*1* person :name "Bob")               :ARG1 (*1* person :name "Jack")
  :ARG1 (*1*))                                   :ARG3 (buy-01
                                                     :ARG1 *1*
                                                     :ARG2 (ice-cream)))
```

Figure 4: Representations of examples (1) and (2) when applying the Indexing method.

referred to (*2* b / buy). The superfluous *2* can simply be removed, but for *3* we have multiple options. Algorithm 1 shows how we handle these cases.

For each referent that was never instantiated, we first check if there is also an instantiated index that is never referred to. If that it is the case, we replace it by that variable. This assumes that the model merely mismatched the index symbols. This works for *3* in Figure 5, even though the resulting node is still incorrect. If that was not the case, we try to replace the referent by an instantiated index that already did have a referent. Since this index already has a referent, we assume it is likely that a mismatched referent actually referred to this index (in Figure 5, *3* would then be replaced by p) . In the case that both previous options failed, we simply pick the variable of the concept that is most often a referent in the training set.

```
(w / want-01                                 (w / want-01
  :ARG1 (*1* p / person :name "Jack")          :ARG1 (p / person :name "Jack")
        :ARG3 (*2* b / buy-01                      :ARG3 (b / buy-01
              :ARG1 (*1*)                                :ARG1 p
              :ARG2 (i / ice-cream)                      :ARG2 (i / ice-cream)
              :ARG3 (*3*)))                              :ARG3 b))
```

Figure 5: Possible output of the model for example (2) on the left, while the fixed AMR after applying Algorithm 1 is shown on the right.

Algorithm 1 Post-processing algorithm used to replace indexes by variables.

R: all referent indexes in output (e.g. *1*, *3*)
X: all instantiated indexes that do not have a referent (e.g. *2* b / buy-01)
Y: all instantiated indexes that have a referent (e.g. *1* person :name "Jack")
C: all concept-variable pairs (e.g. w / want-01)
most_freq: function that, given a list of concepts, selects the concept that is most frequently a referent in the training set

for all ref in R **do**
  if ref $\subseteq$ X **then**
    replace ref by X(ref)
  else if X $\neq \emptyset$ **then**
    replace ref by most_freq(X)
  else if Y $\neq \emptyset$ **then**
    replace ref by most_freq(Y)
  else
    replace ref by most_freq(C)
  end if
end for

Method 3: Absolute Paths In this method reentrancy is established by replacing a co-indexed variable by an absolute path that describes a position within an AMR. Absolute paths start from the top (root) of the AMR. The examples in Figure 6 show the relative paths. In the first AMR, the path `:ARG0` describes that the node refers to the value of the relation `:ARG0`. In the second AMR, the path `:ARG1` refers in a similar way to `:ARG1`. Note that although these examples are straightforward, the paths can become quite long for larger AMRs, e.g. `:op1 :ARG0 :ARG0-of :mod`. The longest path in the training set even contains 14 relations.

```
(like-01
  :ARG0 (person :name "Bob")
  :ARG1 {:ARG0})
```

```
(want-01
  :ARG1 (person :name "Jack")
     :ARG3 (buy-01
           :ARG1 {:ARG1}
           :ARG2 (ice-cream)))
```

Figure 6: Representations of examples (1) and (2) when applying the Absolute Paths method.

This method is perhaps the most attractive from a theoretical point of view. Note, however, that not every node in an AMR can be described by a unique path, as ambiguities might occur when there are two edges with the same name (this can occur, for instance, when more than one modifier is present). To solve these ambiguities an index (e.g. |1|, |2|) is added to each relation in the path.[3] This was necessary for 632 out of the 40,582 paths in the training set. In total, there are 5,760 unique paths, of which 3,447 only occur once. The most frequent path is `:ARG0|1|`, occurring 5,405 times.

Similar to the Indexing method, a problem with this approach is the fact that we have no control over what the model will output. Especially for larger AMRs it is likely that the model will output impossible paths without destination. For example, the model might output `:ARG2` instead of `:ARG0` in the left example in Figure 6.

These impossible paths still need to be replaced by a variable to get a valid AMR. The strategy we opt for here is similar to one used in the Indexing method, namely replacing the path by the variable of the concept in the AMR that most frequently has a referent in the training set.

3.2 Neural model

We implement a bidirectional sequence-to-sequence model with general attention that takes characters as input, using the OpenNMT software (Klein et al., 2017). The parameter settings are the same as in van Noord and Bos (2017) and are shown in Table 2. It is trained for 20 epochs, after which the model that performs best on the development set is used to decode the test set.

Table 2: Parameter settings of the seq2seq model, as in van Noord and Bos (2017).

Parameter	Value	Parameter	Value
Layers	2	RNN type	brnn
Nodes	500	Dropout	0.3
Epochs	20	Vocabulary	100–200
Optimizer	sgd	Max length	750
Learning rate	0.1	Beam size	5
Decay	0.7	Replace unk	true

3.3 Experiments

We test the impact of the different methods on two of our earlier models, described in van Noord and Bos (2017). The first is a simple baseline model that only takes the characters into account without any

[3] For clarity, this was omitted in the example in Figure 6.

additional methods to improve performance. This model is referred to as the char-only model.

The second is the approach that produced one of the best results so far in the literature. This model uses POS-tagged input, clusters together groups of characters (super characters) and exploits 100,000 "silver" AMRs that were obtained by using the off-the-shelf AMR parsers CAMR (Wang et al., 2015) and JAMR (Flanigan et al., 2014)[4]. The added AMRs are all CAMR-produced. We must note that CAMR is not particularly keen on outputting coreference, as the 100,000 silver AMRs only produced 18,865 new reentrancy nodes.

The second approach also employs the postprocessing methods Wikification and pruning, as explained in van Noord and Bos (2017). The Wikification step simply adds wiki links to `:name` nodes, since those links were removed in the input. Pruning is used to remove erroneously produced duplicate output. This is a common problem for sequence-to-sequence models, since the model does not keep track of what it has already output. No pre-training or ensemble methods are used for both approaches.

4 Results and Discussion

4.1 Main results

The results of applying our three methods on the baseline and best model are shown in Table 3. All reported numbers are F-scores obtained by using SMATCH (Cai and Knight, 2013). All three methods offer an improvement over the baseline, for both the baseline and the best model. Indexing is the highest scoring method, except for the test set of the best model, since Reentrancy Restoring obtains the same F-score there. Explicitly encoding the absolute paths resulted in an increase over the baseline, but did not outperform both Reentrancy Restoring and Indexing, although only by a small margin.

Table 3: Results of the different methods in comparison to the char-only and best model.

	Char-only		**Best model**	
	Dev	**Test**	**Dev**	**Test**
Baseline	54.8	53.1	69.3	68.0
Reentrancy Restoring	55.7	54.2	70.0	69.0
Indexing	55.9	56.0	70.5	69.0
Absolute Paths	54.9	53.9	70.3	68.7

Table 4: Results for each method on AMRs with (coref) and without (no coref) reentrancy nodes.

	Char-only				**Best model**			
	Coref		**No coref**		**Coref**		**No Coref**	
	Dev	**Test**	**Dev**	**Test**	**Dev**	**Test**	**Dev**	**Test**
Baseline	52.1	50.3	61.6	60.6	66.9	65.1	73.8	74.8
Reentrancy Restoring	53.4	52.0	61.2	60.8	68.3	66.8	73.8	74.8
Indexing	54.2	53.5	60.5	61.6	68.6	66.5	74.8	74.8
Absolute Paths	52.8	51.5	59.6	59.2	68.2	66.3	74.6	74.5

It is interesting to look at whether we indeed improve on parsing AMRs that have co-indexed variables, in comparison to AMRs that do not contain them. This is shown in Table 4. We see that, in general, we indeed only improve on both baselines for AMRs that have co-indexed variables. This is the case for both the dev and the test set. This is the desired scenario: we improve on AMRs with reentrancy, while

[4]Please see van Noord and Bos (2017) for a full explanation of this process.

performance does not decrease on AMRs without reentrancy. Only applying the Absolute Paths method on the baseline model scores lower on the test set on AMRs without reentrancy nodes. Similar to the results in Table 3, Indexing outperforms Reentrancy Restoring for the baseline model, but has similar scores when applied to the best model.

4.2 Detailed analysis

Table 5 shows the how often the model outputs possible paths for the Absolute Paths method. Unfortunately, about 50% of the time, the model output a path that did not lead to a possible referent, leaving us to rely on the frequency heuristic. This problem is not as severe for our best model, though, since about 75% of paths were actually possible. The addition of extra (silver) data thus helped the model in learning the paths, suggesting that the baseline results might merely be an effect of sparse data. However, the very long paths still proved to be challenging for the best model. This might mean that, even when adding more gold data, learning such sophisticated structures is too difficult for end-to-end sequence-to-sequence models in general.

Table 5: Number of possible (pos) and impossible (imp) paths in the output, for the dev and test set for both our models, when using the Absolute Paths method.

	Char-only				**Best model**			
	Dev		Test		Dev		Test	
	Pos	Imp	Pos	Imp	Pos	Imp	Pos	Imp
Total paths produced	455	464	534	533	636	200	783	328
Paths of length 1	160	30	148	32	231	12	193	13
Paths of length 2	211	202	265	194	268	68	398	108
Paths of length 3	76	156	106	210	130	80	167	123
Paths of length >3	8	76	15	97	7	40	25	84

Table 6 shows more detailed results of the Indexing method. In the majority of cases, the model does what it is supposed to do: first instantiating an index, then referring to it. However, for finding the correct variable replacement for the baseline model, we still have to fall back on heuristics in approximately 30% of the cases. Most of these instances are then solved by referring to the concept that is most frequently a referent in the training set. However, for our best model, this reliance is not there anymore. The model generally only outputs an index when it was instantiated first, which is exactly what was intended.

Table 6: Number of times each step in Algorithm 1 was responsible for replacing an index in the output when using the Indexing method.

	Char-only		**Best model**	
Replace index by	**# Dev**	**# Test**	**# Dev**	**# Test**
Variable that was instantiated	749	984	770	1,122
Variable that was instantiated but not referred to	25	28	0	0
Variable of most frequent instantiated index	8	8	3	9
Variable of most frequent concept	248	217	3	10

5 Conclusion

We proposed three methods to handle co-indexed variables for neural semantic (AMR) parsing. The best results were obtained by the Indexing method, which explicitly encodes co-indexing nodes in the data set. The perhaps theoretically most attractive Absolute Paths performed the worst, although it did still offer an improvement over the baseline. Perhaps an interesting direction for future research is to use relative instead of absolute paths, encoding the path relative to the reentrancy node instead of starting at the top of the AMR, because this will make the paths shorter and more local.

Acknowledgements

We thank the two anonymous reviewers for their comments. We also used a Tesla K40 GPU, which was kindly donated to us by the NVIDIA Corporation. We would also like to thank the Center for Information Technology of the University of Groningen for their support and for providing access to the Peregrine high performance computing cluster. This work was funded by the NWO-VICI grant "Lost in Translation — Found in Meaning" (288-89-003).

References

Banarescu, L., C. Bonial, S. Cai, M. Georgescu, K. Griffitt, U. Hermjakob, K. Knight, P. Koehn, M. Palmer, and N. Schneider (2013, August). Abstract meaning representation for sembanking. In *Proceedings of the 7th Linguistic Annotation Workshop and Interoperability with Discourse*, Sofia, Bulgaria, pp. 178–186. Association for Computational Linguistics.

Barzdins, G. and D. Gosko (2016, June). Riga at semeval-2016 task 8: Impact of smatch extensions and character-level neural translation on amr parsing accuracy. In *Proceedings of the 10th International Workshop on Semantic Evaluation (SemEval-2016)*, San Diego, California. Association for Computational Linguistics.

Buys, J. and P. Blunsom (2017, July). Robust incremental neural semantic graph parsing. In *Proceedings of the 55th Annual Meeting of the Association for Computational Linguistics (Volume 1: Long Papers)*, Vancouver, Canada, pp. 1215–1226. Association for Computational Linguistics.

Cai, S. and K. Knight (2013, August). Smatch: an evaluation metric for semantic feature structures. In *Proceedings of the 51st Annual Meeting of the Association for Computational Linguistics (Volume 2: Short Papers)*, Sofia, Bulgaria, pp. 748–752. Association for Computational Linguistics.

Damonte, M., S. B. Cohen, and G. Satta (2017, April). An incremental parser for abstract meaning representation. In *Proceedings of the 15th Conference of the European Chapter of the Association for Computational Linguistics: Volume 1, Long Papers*, Valencia, Spain, pp. 536–546. Association for Computational Linguistics.

Flanigan, J., S. Thomson, J. Carbonell, C. Dyer, and N. A. Smith (2014, June). A discriminative graph-based parser for the abstract meaning representation. In *Proceedings of the 52nd Annual Meeting of the Association for Computational Linguistics (Volume 1: Long Papers)*, Baltimore, Maryland, pp. 1426–1436. Association for Computational Linguistics.

Foland, W. and J. H. Martin (2017, July). Abstract meaning representation parsing using lstm recurrent neural networks. In *Proceedings of the 55th Annual Meeting of the Association for Computational Linguistics (Volume 1: Long Papers)*, Vancouver, Canada, pp. 463–472. Association for Computational Linguistics.

Klein, G., Y. Kim, Y. Deng, J. Senellart, and A. Rush (2017, July). Opennmt: Open-source toolkit for neural machine translation. In *Proceedings of ACL 2017, System Demonstrations*, Vancouver, Canada, pp. 67–72. Association for Computational Linguistics.

Konstas, I., S. Iyer, M. Yatskar, Y. Choi, and L. Zettlemoyer (2017). Neural amr: Sequence-to-sequence models for parsing and generation. *arXiv preprint (accepted in ACL-2017) arXiv:1704.08381.*

Peng, X., C. Wang, D. Gildea, and N. Xue (2017, April). Addressing the data sparsity issue in neural amr parsing. In *Proceedings of the 15th Conference of the European Chapter of the Association for Computational Linguistics: Volume 1, Long Papers*, Valencia, Spain, pp. 366–375. Association for Computational Linguistics.

Pust, M., U. Hermjakob, K. Knight, D. Marcu, and J. May (2015). Parsing english into abstract meaning representation using syntax-based machine translation. *Training 10*, 218–021.

van Noord, R. and J. Bos (2017). Neural semantic parsing by character-based translation: Experiments with abstract meaning representations. *Accepted in CLiN journal, arXiv preprint arXiv:1705.09980.*

Wang, C., N. Xue, and S. Pradhan (2015, May–June). A transition-based algorithm for amr parsing. In *Proceedings of the 2015 Conference of the North American Chapter of the Association for Computational Linguistics: Human Language Technologies*, Denver, Colorado, pp. 366–375. Association for Computational Linguistics.

Association for Computational Linguistics
209 N. Eighth Street
Stroudsburg, Pennsylvania 18360

ISBN 978-1-5108-5300-3

9 781510 853003

CURRAN ASSOCIATES INC.
proceedings.com